The

Chicks with Sticks®

GUIDE TO

Knitting

The

Chicks with Sticks®

GUIDE TO

Knitting

(*Learn to knit with more than thirty cool, easy patterns*)

Nancy Queen and Mary Ellen O'Connell

WATSON-GUPTILL PUBLICATIONS / NEW YORK

Dedication

To Dan, Dave, and Hadley.

And special thanks to our husbands, Chris & Ben, for their unwavering support.

Acknowledgments

Joy Aquilino & Amy Vinchesi, our editors:

Thanks for keeping us on our toes.

Designer and photo shoot art director Chin-Yee Lai and photographer Simon Lee:

Thanks for making our garments (and us) look good.

To our models, Neena Taylor, Natalie Juliana, and Brad Dickson, for graciously giving their time and bringing our projects to life.

And a VERY special thanks to our customers for their daily encouragement, support, and—most of all—enthusiasm!

Text and project designs copyright © 2008 by Nancy Queen and Mary Ellen O'Connell
Photographs and illustrations copyright © 2008 by Watson-Guptill Publications

First published in 2008 by Watson-Guptill Publications,
Crown Publishing Group, a division of Random House Inc.,
www.crownpublishing.com
www.watsonguptill.com

Watson-Guptill Publications books are available at special discounts when purchased in bulk for premiums and sales promotions. as well as for fund-raising or educational use. Special editions or book excerpts can be created to specification. For details, please contact the Special Sales Director at the address above.

Library of Congress Cataloging-in-Publication Data

Queen, Nancy.
  The Chicks with Sticks' guide to knitting : learn to knit with more than thirty cool, easy patterns / by Nancy Queen and Mary Ellen O'Connell.
     p. cm.
  Includes index.
  ISBN-13: 978-0-8230-0675-5 (pbk. : alk. paper)
  ISBN-10: 0-8230-0675-1 (pbk. : alk. paper)
1. Knitting—Patterns. I. O'Connell, Mary Ellen. II. Title. III. Title: Guide to knitting.
  TT825.Q5164 2008
  746.43'2—dc22

                              2008009603

Executive Editor: Joy Aquilino
Development Editor: Amy Vinchesi
Art Director: Timothy Hsu
Designer: Chin-Yee Lai
Photo Shoot Art Director: Chin-Yee Lai
Photographer: Simon Lee
Illustrators: Carmen Galiano (instructional) and Sivan Earnest (schematic)
Production Director: Alyn Evans

Printed in China

First printing, 2008

2 3 4 5 6 7 8 9 / 15 14 13 12 11 10 09

Contents

Introduction

WELCOME TO NO FEAR, NO SWEAT, NO PROBLEM KNITTING

This is our philosophy of how to learn to knit in the fastest, easiest way possible! You will learn to knit a little bit at a time and practice each technique with an interesting project. You won't feel overwhelmed with projects that are too complicated; instead you'll discover projects that keep your hands busy, your mind a little challenged, and your soul satisfied.

It is always a little intimidating when you try something new. We take the fear out of learning to knit by providing you with terms and projects that are easy to master. Often we see beginners jump into projects that are too difficult; and they end up feeling overwhelmed and frustrated, and quit before they even start. You won't feel that way with this book!

KNITTING PAST

Remember those stiff, itchy wool sweaters Grandma used to knit? They were so thick that you could live on the Arctic tundra and still be hot wearing them, and your mittens were so tight you couldn't bend your fingers! Projects back then were completed on the tiniest needles and often with lots of intricate stitches and complex color changes. There weren't many yarn choices available either. They had wool in two-ply or four-ply, and mohair was considered "novelty."

KNITTING PRESENT—NOT YOUR GRANDMA'S KNITTING!

Times have changed and so has knitting! Today's knitter isn't huddled in a rocking chair passing the time. More and more people, including celebrities, are picking up sticks and knitting. It is now hip to knit. You'll find knitting clubs in schools and on college campuses, knitting blogs and groups on the Internet, as well as many online yarns stores.

Knitting today has evolved to be a portable, uncomplicated, and very sociable hobby. Advances in technology and our busy lifestyles play key roles in those changes. New machining and fibers have allowed yarn manufacturers to produce yarns like never before: softer wools; richer colors; interesting blends; and more fun, funky novelty yarn. Our fast-paced lives have compelled us to knit in such places as carpool lines, at the doctor's office, on the train or plane, or wherever we can spare a moment for ourselves.

KNITTING FUTURE

Living in a "fast food" society, we have become accustomed to receiving instant gratification and buying, buying, buying. Knitting will slow down your life a little, remind you of a simpler time, help you relax and reenergize, and provide you with a sense of satisfaction that you just can't get from buying something. You'll get to see the material in its raw form and then watch it turn into something wonderful that you've created with your own two hands. Your abilities in knitting will be as limitless as your imagination.

Are You Destined for Knitting? Take a Quick Quiz!

1. Are you looking for something to spark your creativity?
2. Do you have a lot of stress in your life?
3. Do you get stuck waiting in lines, at sporting events, on travel commutes, and in doctors' offices with nothing to do?
4. Are you a do-it-yourselfer and love the feeling of making something by hand?
5. Do you like to meet people with a passion for the same hobby?
6. Do you like to make cool stuff?

If you answered yes to most of these questions, you are destined to be a knitter.

KNITTING A GO-GO

Knitting is portable, so you can take it with you anywhere you go. We named ourselves "The Chicks with Sticks" because, quite frankly, you will never find us without our hooks and needles. We are addicted, and you'll find us at the next YA (Yarn-o-holics Anonymous) meeting proclaiming it proudly. Like you, we are busy gals but love the chance to kick off our shoes, put up our feet, and get those fingers moving. We enjoy projects where we don't necessarily have to pay too much attention because we are also busy gabbing, or we don't want to miss who-did-what on our favorite TV show. Most important, knitting is something we love! It's easy to learn and a lot of fun to do. We want you to be able to enjoy it as much as we do; and, hopefully, you'll teach others how to knit.

Top 10 Reasons Why You'll LOVE This Book!

1. Updated, yet timeless patterns and projects.

2. Projects that are easy yet not juvenile.

3. Patterns that use repetitive stitches or easy color changes, allowing you to relax and knit.

4. Step-by-step instructions that guide you through the knitting process; one lesson builds upon the next.

5. Fun, relaxing projects that may have an interesting stitch repeat to keep you on your toes but that are not so complex you can't take your eyes off them for a second.

6. Added information to help you select the right yarn and tools for knitting.

7. Helpful hints and tricks not usually covered in instruction books.

8. The confidence boost you'll feel when you complete a lesson.

9. The knowledge that you're not alone in this; we've included ideas on how to put more knitting and knitters in your life.

10. We'll turn you into a Chick with Sticks in no time!

HOW THIS BOOK IS SET UP

The Chicks with Sticks Guide to Knitting is arranged in lessons to help you learn knitting step-by-step, with each lesson providing building blocks for the next lessons. The first lesson will familiarize you with knitting needles, tools, and yarns, as well as how to read yarn labels and patterns. The next few lessons introduce you to knitting and purling. With each new lesson we've incorporated projects for you to test out your new skills. As the lessons advance, you will learn more complex stitches and how to do felting, and even get to try your hand at sweaters. We'll teach you our secrets for the best knitting results: how to measure yourself for the best-fitting garment; how to select yarns; and how to make garment shaping effortless by doing our Chicks' Knitting Shorthand. Finally, we wrap up the book with how to meet other knitters in your community, start a knitting club, and even share your hobby with charitable knitting. Bring your perseverance and enthusiasm, and let's get started!

Cheep Tricks

The Chicks are all about shortcuts. We like to find the easiest, yet most effective way to do stuff. So we've added some of our favorite Cheep Tricks throughout the book to help you learn the ins and outs of knitting often not mentioned in a book or pattern.

Chick Feed

With each pattern you'll find a little Chick Feed. These tidbits of info let you know why we created each design to accompany a lesson and what skills you will master.

Fly the Coop!

If the increased knitting confidence you will gain after completing a lesson gives you the desire to "wing it," you'll like Fly the Coop! These are additional ideas to individualize your project, such as easy ways to alter the pattern, add embellishment, or use yarn alternatives. It will help spark your creativity and allow endless possibilities for each project.

TOOLS AND TACKLE

~~~~~~

Needles, Needles, and More Needles

Knitting needles are the main tools you will use in knitting. Just as an artist uses different paintbrushes to achieve varied strokes and textures in a painting, you will use different knitting needles. You will begin with the most basic straight needles and gradually advance to other sizes and styles as your skills progress. This section will familiarize you with the basic terms and give an overview of the needles as tools; you'll be introduced to the needles themselves later on in the projects.

SIZE DOES MATTER

Needles come in a variety of widths, from skinny as a toothpick to thick as a broomstick. The varying widths will determine how large the stitches are. Simply put, the smaller the needles, the smaller the stitches; the larger the needles, the larger the stitches. Most needles today are measured in US standard sizes and millimeters. However, over the years different countries have adopted their own needle-sizing standards. The chart opposite will help make sense of the needle size standards.

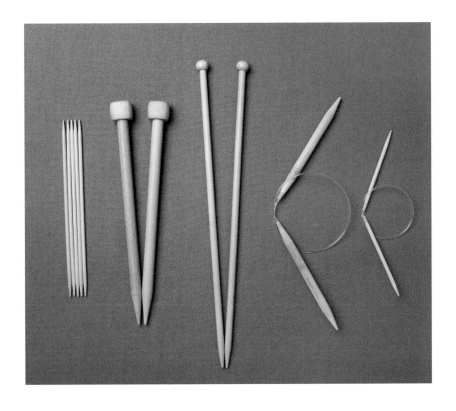

Straight Needles

Straight needles, for flat-panel knitting, come in a variety of materials: metal, bamboo, wood, and plastic. Everyone has an opinion on his or her favorite needles; and, take it from us, each person will swear by that preference. We find that certain needles work better for different types of yarn. For example, bamboo needles are very smooth without being slippery and will give you great control with today's novelty yarns. Metal needles let your stitches glide effortlessly when working with traditional yarns.

Circular Needles

Circular needles have a short, single-pointed needle at each end that is connected by a flexible cord in between. They come in several different lengths and are used to knit in a circle, thereby creating seamless fabric. They can also be used for knitting flat pieces by knitting back and forth, as with straight needles.

Knitting Needle Conversion Chart

US	Metric
0	2 mm
1	2 1/4 mm
	2 1/2 mm
2	2 3/4 mm
	3 mm
3	3 1/4 mm
4	3 1/2 mm
5	3 3/4 mm
6	4 mm
7	4 1/2 mm
8	5 mm
9	5 1/2 mm
10	6 mm
10 1/2	6 1/2 mm
	7 mm
	7 1/2 mm
11	8 mm
13	9 mm
15	10 mm

Double-Pointed Needles

Double-pointed needles are exactly as they sound, needles with a point at either end. They are used to work in the round, as with circular needles, but with these you can knit from both ends. Double-points are used when the circumference of the piece you are knitting is too small to work comfortably on a circular needle. Smaller projects, such as socks, hats, mittens, and gloves, are usually worked on double-pointed needles. They are often sold in packages of four or five, depending on the brand; this enables you to have three or four needles to hold your stitches and one working needle. Beginning knitters are usually wary of these pointy, weaponlike needles, but never fear: Later in the book we will introduce some patterns that will make the transition painless.

CHEEP TRICKS

Needles come in so many lengths and sizes, only someone with a photographic memory could be expected to remember them all. The solution? Stash in your purse a little card with the needle sizes you already own so that the next time you find a project you just have to knit, you won't end up buying the same needles over and over.

IT'S IN THE BAG: THE CHICKS' TOOLS CHECKLIST

As you begin your first project you'll probably only need knitting needles, yarn, scissors, and a finishing needle to weave in the yarn ends. But here are some of the tools we recommend as you progress and what they are used for:

- **Scissors** ~ Keep a nice sharp pair on hand for trimming yarn ends.
- **Stitch holders** ~ Available in different lengths, they are used to hold "live stitches" (stitches that are on the needle) that are not being worked at the time. Stitches are slipped onto the stitch holder, where they are held until they need to be worked. When necessary, the stitches are knitted off the holder.
- **Crochet hook** ~ A handy tool that can be used for making fringe, picking up dropped stitches and working a single crochet edge to finish a garment edge.
- **Row counters** ~ Used to keep track of your rows in knitting. It is especially important to keep track of increased and decreased rows. We totally depend on counters because they take the guesswork out of where you are in your project, especially when you put your work down and then pick it up again.
- **Notepad and pen/pencil** ~ As you work through the lessons in this book you will find that there is a lot of information to remember. Just keep a notepad and pencil handy to jot down things, such as where you are in a project in case you need to put it down, thoughts on an interesting stitch you want to try, or notes on mapping out your projects (we'll talk more about that in a later lesson).
- **Finishing needle** ~ Looks just like a giant sewing needle, with a blunt end and a large eye that the yarn will fit through easily. These needles are used to sew your projects together and to weave in loose yarn ends.
- **Stitch markers** ~ Round rings that are slipped onto your needle in between stitches, they basically serve the same purpose as tying a string around your finger to remind you to do something. They can be used to mark the beginning of rounds, spots for increasing or decreasing stitches, or where a stitch change is needed in a row.
- **Tape measure** ~ Handy to have for measuring garment length, checking your gauge, etc.
- **Stitch gauge** ~ Like a small ruler, but a stitch gauge usually has a little box cut out, and stitches are counted inside it.

CHEEP TRICKS

There are several ways to keep track of your knitting rows; hand-held counters that you manually click through are the Chicks' favorite. There is also a counter that has a dial and sits on the end of your needle. Or you can just keep track the old-fashioned way—with a pencil and paper. Whatever method you choose, make sure you decide at the out-set whether you are counting at the start or end of a row. And here's a tip we learned the hard way: When using a handheld counter, it's best to keep it out of reach of curious kiddies who like to play with anything that has small buttons! So, for safety's sake, when you leave your knit-ting, always write down what number row you ended on some-where on the pattern.

● **Cable needle** ~ A small, funny-looking needle with points at either end that is usually about 4″ long and has a shallow, U-shaped dip in the middle. Another variation is shaped like a deep J. Cable needles are used to temporarily hold any stitches that you've taken off your working needle that will be worked later. Stitches on the cable needle are held either in the front or in back of your work (the pattern will direct you where to hold them); the stitches are then picked up off the cable needle at the appropriate point.

Yarn Ho! The Lure of Yarn

The best part of knitting is the yarn. Crocheting and knitting have recently encountered a renaissance, thanks in part to technological advances in the yarn world. New machinery produces exciting yarns mixed with bobbles, fringes, and a seemingly endless combination of fibers. Innovative chemicals and creative spinning processes produce techno yarns; microfibers; Tence; viscose; and softer wools, alpacas, and mohair. Agricultural advancements have generated yarns made from bamboo, soy, and corn, and have resulted in more refined cottons and linens. This section is an overview of all things yarn: how yarn is wound (aka "put up"); how to read a yarn label; and yarn weight, colors, and fibers.

CHEEP TRICKS
Don't try to knit directly from an unwound hank. This yarn must first be wound into a ball. Some yarn shops will wind the yarn for you, or you can place the yarn around the back of a chair and carefully wind it into a ball.

HANK, BALL, SKEIN? UNRAVELING YARN LINGO

If you've been "hankering" to learn the language of yarn, here's the lowdown. Yarn is packaged in three ways: hanks, balls, or skeins (left to right, above).

- A **hank** is wound in a long loop. Many hand-dyed and luxury yarns are packaged this way.
- A **ball** is just what it sounds like, a ball shape.
- A **skein** (pronounced *skeyn*) is a longer, machine-wound bundle.

The Skein Game

Which end of the yarn do I pull? Years ago, it used to be that most skeins of yarn were wound on standard machinery, and you could pull from the center. Today, as the yarns available to us have vastly improved, so has the machinery. Most balls and skeins now pull from the outside. It's a good idea to keep your yarn in a tote or basket to keep it from rolling around on the floor.

THE 411 ON YARN LABELS

There is a lot of valuable information on a yarn label. It's a good idea to keep a journal or notebook of your projects and include the yarn label for reference.

* **Name of the Yarn** ~ Helpful to know if you ever want to knit with the yarn again or need to purchase more to finish your project.
* **Name of the Yarn Manufacturer** ~ Believe it or not, there are hundreds of yarn manufacturers and distributors. Often they choose the same names for their yarns, so it is a good idea to know the name of the company as well as the name of the yarn.
* **Fiber Content** ~ Knowing what the yarn is spun from will help you predict the drape of the finished garment and how to care for it. Check to make sure it is not an allergenic fiber for the wearer (some people have wool or silk allergies, for example) and to see if it's appropriate for the project you have in mind.
* **Weight** ~ The weight is usually given in grams or ounces (and sometimes both), and this helps determine how much yarn is needed for a project. Most yarns come in 50- to 100-gram balls or skeins. Years ago, before there was such a large variety of yarn available, patterns were written noting how many grams or ounces of yarn were needed to complete a project. Since there are so many different thicknesses of yarn available today, one 50-gram ball of yarn may have only 58 yards to a ball while another ball of the same weight may have more than 200 yards to a ball. Today, most patterns will note the yardage and the yarn thickness rather than the yarn weight to determine how much yarn is needed.
* **Yardage** ~ This is some of the most important information on the label. It helps you determine how much yarn you need to complete a project. Some labels note the yardage in yards while others give the information in meters. Most patterns will tell you how much yarn you need for your project in yards. Here is a quick way to figure out a conversion in your head. These measurements aren't exact, but they do the trick!
  * To convert yards to meters, subtract 10%. For example, if the ball is 100 yards, 10% is 10 yards, so your total is roughly 90 meters.
  * To convert meters to yards, add 10%. For example, if the ball is 100 meters, 10% is 10 meters, so your total is roughly 110 yards.

Color Code and **Dye Lot Number** ~ Yarn shades are usually assigned a color code and a dye lot number. A batch of yarn dyed at the same time will have the same dye lot number. When manufacturers dye yarn, especially hand-dye, the color can vary quite a bit from batch to batch. When you purchase the yarn for a project, it is important to check the dye lot number on each ball of yarn to make sure all of the balls are from the same lot. If not, you could end up with a patch in the middle of your garment where the odd ball was used.

Care Instructions ~ Most yarn labels use standard international care instructions. Here are the most common ones you'll see:

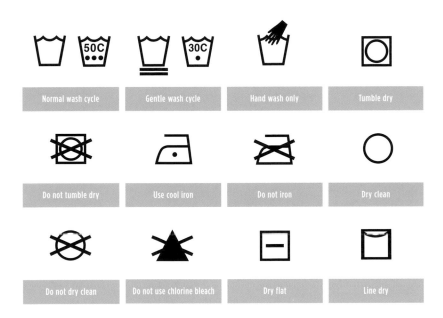

Normal wash cycle	Gentle wash cycle	Hand wash only	Tumble dry
Do not tumble dry	Use cool iron	Do not iron	Dry clean
Do not dry clean	Do not use chlorine bleach	Dry flat	Line dry

Tension (Gauge) and **Needle Size** ~ This is the yarn label that indicates the tension, or gauge, the yarn manufacturer suggests for a particular yarn, and it will usually note how many stitches are worked over 1" or over 4". The label also notes the needle size used to get that gauge. This information is just a reference point for determining whether the yarn will work with the project you want to make.

GET THE SKINNY ON YARN WEIGHT

Yarns come in a variety of weights, which simply means the thickness of the yarn. The weights are determined by how many stitches it takes to knit over 4″. Generally speaking, the thinner the yarn, the more stitches per inch; the thicker the yarn, the fewer stitches per inch.

* **Lace** weight yarns are the thinnest of the bunch and are usually knitted on larger needle for lacy, openwork patterns.
* **Fine** and **Super Fine** weight yarns are most often used for intricate projects such as socks, baby garments, and lace, to name a few.
* **Light Worsted** or **DK** weight yarns are thicker than fingering weight yarn but not as thick as worsted. They are usually used for summer weight garments, shawls, and baby items.
* **Medium Weight** (aka **Worsted** and **Aran** weight yarns), are the most popular thickness and are commonly used for sweaters, blankets, hats, mittens, and many felting projects.
* **Bulky** and **Super Bulky** weight yarns are the thickest of the group. Some, at one stitch per inch, are often suggested for sweaters, scarves, afghans, and more. If you want a really fast project, then patterns requiring these yarns will most likely be the ones you want to head for.

CHEEP TRICKS
Always try to match your yarn weight and fiber content to those called for in the pattern.

This information is not ironclad, but it is helpful to give a range so you can head toward the right weight when choosing a yarn to go with a specific pattern you want to knit.

 Lace: Fingering 10-count crochet thread (33–40 stitches to 4″)

 Super Fine: Sock, fingering, and baby weight yarns (27–32 stitches to 4″)

 Fine: Sport, baby weight yarns (23–26 stitches to 4″)

 Light: DK, light worsted weight yarns (21–24 stitches to 4″)

 Medium: Worsted, afghan, aran weight yarns (16–20 stitches to 4″)

 Bulky: Chunky, craft weight yarns (12–15 stitches to 4″)

 Super Bulky: Bulky, roving weight yarns (6–11 stitches to 4″)

Adapted from the Standard Yarn Weight System of the Craft Yarn Council of America.

FEEL THE LOVE: THE CHICKS LOVE FIBERS

The art of knitting is all about the fiber. As you will soon find out, *nothing* feels better than yarn. Choosing just the right material for your project can make all the difference in its final look. A sweater knitted in cashmere, for example, is going to have a completely different drape than one made out of mohair, silk, or even acrylic. Getting familiar with the properties of the particular fibers will help you choose just the right fiber for your project.

Natural Animal Fibers

* **Wool** Spun into a wide variety of thicknesses and textures, wool, which is provided by several different breeds of sheep, has long been a popular fiber for knitters because it is warm and breathable, accepts dye well, and is very resilient.
* **Cashmere** This fiber comes from the soft undercoat of cashmere goats. It's an ultraluxury yarn that is very soft, light, and warm.
* **Alpaca** The coats of these South American animals produce very soft, silky, and luxurious yarn. The softest comes from baby alpacas. The allergens found in the lanolin in lamb's wool are nonexistent in alpaca, making it a great choice for those with wool allergies. The Chicks' best-kept secret: Since alpaca doesn't have the "street credibility" of cashmere, it is usually about one-third the price.
* **Llama** tends to be a bit coarser than alpaca and is often used for bulkier (and warmer) garments. Like alpaca, it is nonallergenic and lanolin-free. It is available in twenty-two natural shades but doesn't accept dye as easily as wool.
* **Mohair** Provided by the Angora goat, mohair is a very lofty and fuzzy yarn that is usually crocheted very loosely and provides a lot of warmth. The finest mohair is kid mohair.
* **Silk** Produced by silkworm larvae, it is light, smooth, and comfortable. There are many types of silkworms that produce different types of silk. Since silk does not have much stretch, it is hard to knit with it alone; it is usually combined with other fibers such as wool or cashmere.
* Other interesting animal fibers that are available in yarn include **Angora**, **camel**, and **buffalo**.

Natural Plant Fibers

* **Cotton** The use of this material in garments dates back to ancient times. Breathable and absorbent yarn, it is ideal for hot weather. Mercerized cotton is treated with chemicals to make it shinier, silkier, and more durable. This also allows the cotton to accept dyes better and makes it mildew resistant.
* **Bamboo** is the new kid on the block, made from the pulp of the bamboo grass. It has a drape similar to silk—light and strong—and is nonallergenic.
* **Linen** comes from the flax plant. Cool and moisture resistant, it is great for summer clothing.

Man-made Fibers

Man-made fibers and those created by way of chemical processes include nylon, viscose, rayon, acrylic, and polyester. Man-made fibers, also known as synthetics, aren't as undesirable as they once were, but technological improvements have paved the way for synthetics to be softer, accept dye better, and pill less. Some yarns are composed of natural fibers—the cellulose from plants—and then turned into yarn using man-made processes. Some of these "techno fibers" include rayon, viscose, and even corn fiber.

Blends

Blends are a combination of different types of natural and/or man-made yarns. These yarns take the best properties from both yarns and combine them to make something completely fabulous. You may find a silk/wool blend or a cotton/acrylic blend. Try working with a few different types of blends—you may end up liking them more than pure yarns.

CHOOSING YARN COLORS

The range of colors available today has never been greater. This feast for the eyes is usually what draws a person to a particular yarn. Everyone perceives color a bit differently. And just as some favor chocolate ice cream over vanilla, there are many "flavors" of yarn to suit your taste.

Which Comes First, the Pattern or the Yarn?

Like the age-old chicken-and-egg dilemma, where do you start when looking for a project? Go into a yarn shop and browse. Anything can spark your imagination—a beautiful color, the drape of a wrap, an interesting stitch, or the styling of a sweater. No one way to shop for a project is right or wrong; you will develop the best way that works for you. Sometimes you find a yarn you just have to work with, so you search for a pattern to do it justice. Other times you find a pattern you adore and seek out the right yarn to coordinate with it.

The options! The possibilities! This artistic process is an exciting step in knitting. Learn to let your creative juices flow!

The Chicks Know How to Buy Yarn

1. Start by narrowing down the yarns with the correct gauge for your project.

2. Walk around and choose a color that catches your eye. If it's going to be a garment for you, hold up the yarn to your face and look in a mirror to make sure it's a good color for your complexion.

3. Get hands-on—feel the yarn and fall in love with the texture.

4. Make sure the care instructions are appropriate for the planned project.

5. Buy one more ball than the pattern suggests to make sure you don't run out.

6. Check the dye lot numbers to make sure they are all the same.

7. Buy the best yarn you can afford. Now, we're not saying you should knit every item out of cashmere, but there is a difference in the quality of yarns. Treat yourself on occasion to some of the finer fibers. Remember, you are going to spend a lot of time and energy working on a project. You want to enjoy the finished product, so why not use a yarn you really love?

8. You can never have too much yarn.

A Note on Yarns Used in This Book

Yarn is a lot like fashion. Some yarns are traditional and some are trendy. Some yarns have been around for fifty years (from back when Grandma knitted) while others hang around for only a few seasons. While writing this book, we tried to stick with some of the more traditional yarns in hopes that they will be available for quite a while. However, trends change, and some yarns are eventually discontinued and replaced by newer yarns. In all of the designs, we noted not only the name of the yarn and the manufacturer, but also the yarn content and the gauge. This will allow you to substitute yarns, if necessary.

. . . .

Knitting Patterns: Recipes for Success

Imagine you are about to bake a cake. You need to follow a recipe, use the right ingredients, measure for the right serving size, and set the proper oven temperature in order for the cake to come out properly. Now consider your knitting pattern the same way. To make it work, you'll need the right materials, the correct gauge, accurate measurements, and an understanding of the instructions for a successful outcome.

- The "recipe" (skill level): Is the pattern designed for an apprentice or a master chef?
- What "ingredients" (materials) will you need to whip up this tasty morsel?
- "Serving size" (completed measurements): Make the right amount for the number of guests or, in the case of a knitting pattern, the right size garment for the wearer.
- What "temperature" (gauge) will the chef use to bake the cake? Remember, just as temperature varies from oven to oven, gauge varies from knitter to knitter!
- Finally, follow the instructions for putting it all together. Just as baking may have some interesting terms and abbreviations, so does knitting. Once you become accustomed to reading knitting lingo and schematics, the better "chef" knitter you'll be!

Skill Level

Projects are usually assigned a skill level. Oftentimes we see knitters dive (or get pushed) into projects that are too difficult. They get overwhelmed and frustrated and give up a great hobby before they've had a chance to enjoy it. All of the designs in this book are Beginner or Advanced Beginner. They are easy not because we want to insult your intelligence (after all, you were smart enough to buy this book!). They are easy because we want you to be able to master each technique before moving on to the next. You'll find you'll make fewer mistakes, work faster, and become more confident in your work if you take it step by step.

How Do I Know My Skill Level?

While we stick to Beginner and Advanced Beginner patterns in this book, here are some of the skill ratings you may come across in other patterns:

* **Beginner ~** Projects for first-time knitters. These projects use the Knit stitch (the most basic stitch) and very minimal finishing skills.
* **Advanced Beginner ~** Projects use basic stitches and may include repetitive stitch patterns, simple color changes, and simple shaping and finishing techniques.
* **Intermediate ~** Projects using a variety of techniques, such as basic lace patterns or color changes, midlevel shaping, and finishing techniques.
* **Experienced ~** Projects with intricate stitch patterns, techniques, dimensions such as nonrepeating patterns, multicolor techniques, fine yarns, small needles, detailed shaping, and refined finishing techniques.

Materials

Patterns always indicate what type of yarn was used and how much you will need for your project as well as the recommended needle sizes. See The Chicks' Tools Checklist (page 15) for other materials you will need.

Completed Measurements

Patterns usually include completed measurements for the project. For a bag or scarf this will be the finished length, width, and depth (for bags); for a garment, the finished bust or chest size is usually given. A simple trick is to measure a great-fitting sweater that you already have in your closet and use those measurements as a guide to choosing your size.

Find Your Size

The first few projects in this book do not require sizing. But soon enough you will be knitting garments, and you will find that designers don't always make "one size fits all" patterns; they include several sizes to allow the proper fit. For convenience and to save space, one pattern is written for all sizes. Size changes will be noted in corresponding order throughout the pattern. For example, let's say you want to make a sweater for yourself, and you wear a size medium. The pattern will print size information like this: "Sizes: Small (**Medium**, Large, X-Large)." To match the garment to your size—medium—you will follow the corresponding first number in parentheses throughout the pattern, like so: "Cast on 23 (**25**, 27, 29) sts." So, instead of working 23 stitches (size Small), you work 25 for size Medium, 27 for Large, and so on. It helps to go through the pattern before you begin your project and circle all your size numbers with a pencil. If no varying sizes are noted, this just means that information is the same for all sizes.

Basic Conversions

Inches = Centimeters x 0.39

Yards = Meters x 1.09

Centimeters = Inches x 2.54

Meters = Yards x 0.91

Gauge

The gauge indicates how many stitches and rows were knit by the pattern designer over 4″. It is essential to match the gauge noted so that your project will have the expected outcome, especially when knitting a garment. Read Lesson 6, "Take a Test Drive" (page 60), to learn how to make a test swatch and measure your gauge.

Knitting Lingo

Knitting does use a lot of abbreviations and strange punctuation. This has been done to simplify patterns for both the publisher and the knitter. Most of the symbols are used universally, and once you recognize them they will allow you to read patterns at a glance.

Abbreviations

approx	approximately
beg	beginning
dec	decrease
inc	increase
K	Knit
K2tog	Knit 2 stitches together
m 1	Make 1 (inc)
P	Purl
pm	place marker
sl st	slip stitch
st(s)	stitch(es)
St st	Stockinette stitch
tbl	through back loop
yo	yarn over

Schematics

Schematics are small-scale drawings of a pattern with all the specific measurements. These can be very helpful to the knitter. Schematics are like having small maps to your garment. They allow you to see how the pieces to your project are shaped and the correct measurements for each size. By looking at a schematic, you can visualize the work involved in the project and also know the exact measurements.

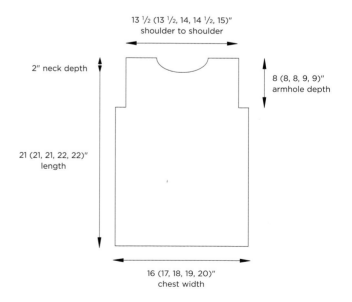

13 ¹/₂ (13 ¹/₂, 14, 14 ¹/₂, 15)″ shoulder to shoulder

2″ neck depth

8 (8, 8, 9, 9)″ armhole depth

21 (21, 21, 22, 22)″ length

16 (17, 18, 19, 20)″ chest width

THE CHICKS' KNITTING CRASH COURSE

What Is Knitting?

Knitting is the age-old art of using two needles and a ball of yarn to create loops, which are joined together to create fabric. Flat-panel knitting is worked back and forth, row by row. Circular knitting, or knitting in the round, is worked by knitting around and around to create tubes or circles.

Rule #1: Don't curb your enthusiasm! If you are anything like us, once you've decided you want to start something, you want the "down and dirty" basics so you can get on your way! The other details will come later. This "crash course" chapter will teach you about making a slip knot, casting on, doing the Knit stitch, binding off, and finishing off. Just by practicing these simple steps you will learn how to make a variety of fun and easy projects that will help you master the art of knitting.

GET A GRIP: HOLDING THE NEEDLES

Two sticks and a ball of yarn; now, what to do with them? In this lesson we will cover how to hold the needles, get the stitches onto the needles, and how to actually make knit stitches. In a nutshell, once you cast the stitches onto the needle, you place the needle in your left hand and then "knit" the stitches onto the right needle. After all the stitches have been knit onto your right needle, you place it back in your left hand and the entire process begins again:

this is knitting! So let's start with how to grasp the needles. Since knitting is a hobby that has been passed down from generation to generation, people around the world have adopted various ways to hold the needles. We are going to cover the two most common ways: the Throw Method and Continental Method. There is no right or wrong way, so simply try both methods and use whichever one feels most comfortable to you.

Throw Method

The Throw, or English, Method is a very common way to knit and is very popular among new knitters because you simply wrap the yarn around the needle to make a stitch. As we mentioned earlier, you will hold one needle in each hand, grasping them as if they are knives and you are ready to cut something. Your right hand will control the yarn and work it around the needles if you are right-handed (1–2). If you are left-handed, your left hand will control the yarn. This method is easily taught and will be the one shown in this book.

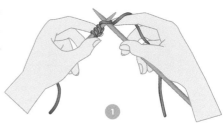

Continental Method

The Continental, or European, Method of knitting requires a bit more skill because you need to maintain consistent tension with the yarn. It tends to be the method of choice for more accomplished knitters because it requires less movement and allows for faster knitting once you get the hang of it. To knit Continental-style you also hold your needles as if they are knives and you are ready to cut, but instead of holding the yarn in your right hand, you will weave the yarn through the fingers of your left hand (right hand if you're a lefty) and keep it somewhat taut. This will allow you to pull up a stitch with your right needle (3). When weaving the yarn through your fingers, find a configuration that feels comfortable to you. It can be a little more difficult to maintain even yarn tension using this method, especially for a beginner, but it can be mastered, if practiced.

Southpaws, Don't Feel Left Out

Lefties, you can knit too! (Take it from Nancy, a fellow southpaw.) Basic stitch information is written the same for both left- and right-handed knitters. More advanced stitch instructions are written for the right-handed knitter, so lefties should just follow the same directions, reversing right and left. For example, if the directions tell you to insert the right-hand needle, you will insert your left-hand needle instead. Another important tip to remember is that southpaws will always wrap their yarn around the needles clockwise (as opposed to counterclockwise for righties).

CONTROL YOURSELF: YARN TENSION

Controlling the tension of the yarn is very important and can be somewhat difficult for a beginning knitter. If you pull it too tightly (as if you were controlling the reins on a team of galloping horses) or if you wrap your yarn too loosely, you will end up with uneven stitches. Holding just the right amount of tension in your yarn does take some getting used to, but the Chicks promise that if you stick with it and keep practicing, you will figure it out in no time at all. Remember what it felt like when we were learning how to write our names as children, how odd and unfamiliar that pencil felt in our hands? It probably feels the same way when holding knitting needles for the first few times. But by using the Three Ps—persistence, patience, and practice—we were pros in no time at all!

CHEEP TRICKS

For your first few projects, it's better if you don't select black or another very dark yarn color because it ends up being too difficult to make out the details of exactly what's happening with your stitches. Choose a brighter yarn, and you won't miss a thing!

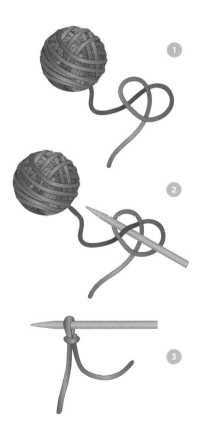

BE A LITTLE KNOTTY: THE SLIP KNOT

The first stitch in creating any knitting project is called a slip knot; it is how you attach the yarn to the needle. The length of the yarn tail you will use to tie the slip knot depends on how many stitches you will be "casting on," which we'll explain next. For now, it's a good rule of thumb to estimate approximately twenty stitches; there may be fewer stitches if you're using a chunky yarn and big needles, or more stitches if you're using a thin yarn and smaller needles. As a general guide, allow approximately three times the planned width of your cast-on row.

1. After you have measured your yarn, make a loop by crossing the yarn closer to the ball over the tail end.
2. Push the yarn through the middle of the loop and place this on your needle.
3. Pull gently on both yarn ends to tighten the loop on the needle. The proper tension allows the loop to slide easily up and down the needle.

CHEEP TRICKS

All projects begin with a slip knot, but this information is not usually stated in a pattern. It is always assumed that you know to start with a slip knot.

CASTING ON

After making a slip knot, you must then create the first row of stitches, which is called casting on. There are more than thirty-five different ways to cast on, but we're going to stick with the basics for now and show you our favorite, known as the long-tail cast-on, because it builds a nice, stable foundation for your stitches and makes it easy to knit your first row. It is known as a long-tail cast-on because rather than making the slip knot right at the end of the ball, you will need to leave a long tail of yarn, and the stitches are formed by using both the tail and the ball of yarn.

Long-Tail Cast-On

1. Make a slip knot but leave a tail that is long enough to accommodate the number of stitches required by your pattern.

2. Holding the needle in your right hand, position the tail toward you and the yarn ball away from you. Place the forefinger and thumb of your left hand between both yarn ends and enclose the ends with the rest of your hand. The yarn will resemble a triangle. Now point your forefinger and thumb upward and angle the needle downward, so that now it resembles a slingshot.

3. Insert the needle underneath the loop on your thumb and then insert the needle through the loop wrapped around your forefinger from the top. Next, flip the loop from your thumb over the needle. This will create one stitch on your needle. Pull gently on the yarn that is attached to the ball to tighten the loop on your needle, remembering that you should be able to slide your stitches up and down the needle easily; this will ensure that you have the correct tension on your stitches.

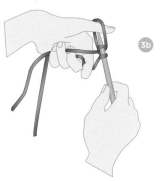

4. Repeat step 3 until you have the required number of stitches on your needle.

5. Transfer the needle with your cast-on stitches to your left hand, and you are ready to begin knitting!

CHEEP TRICKS

We like to break down this cast-on method into a few simple steps to remember; we've found that repeating "thumb, finger, over" in our heads often does the trick. Nancy taught her daughter how to cast on by using this little ditty: "The bunny comes out of the hole, jumps over the fence, and hops back in his hole."

KNIT STITCH

Okay, if you've been following along, you should know how to hold your needles and have your stitches cast on to the needle. So now it's time to take the leap and make your first stitches! We begin with the Knit stitch. All other stitches are built upon or are a variation of the Knit stitch. Simply put, the Knit stitch is a method of wrapping yarn around the needle to form loops to make a piece of fabric.

Here's how it's done:

1. Hold the needle with your cast-on stitches in your left hand, with the yarn held in back. Insert the right-hand needle in the first stitch from front to back.
2. Wrap the yarn around the right-hand needle counterclockwise; the yarn now will be between both needles.
3. Using the right-hand needle, catch the yarn and pull it forward through the stitch on the left-hand needle; slip the stitch off the left-hand needle, leaving a new stitch on the right-hand needle.
4. Repeat these steps until all the newly formed stitches are on the right-hand needle.
5. Start the next row by moving the needle that is holding the stitches to your left hand and the empty needle to your right hand. Repeat steps 1–4.

Tah-dah! You may now officially call yourself a knitter!

Knit Stitch for Southpaws

1. Hold the needle with your cast-on stitches in your right hand, with the yarn held in back. Insert the left-hand needle in the first stitch from front to back.
2. Wrap the yarn around the left-hand needle clockwise. The yarn now will be between both needles.
3. Using the left-hand needle, catch the yarn and pull it forward through the stitch on the right-hand needle; slip the stitch off the right-hand needle, leaving a new stitch on the left-hand needle.
4. Repeat these steps until all the newly formed stitches are on the left-hand needle.
5. Start the next row by moving the needle that is holding the stitches to your right hand and the empty needle to your left hand. Repeat steps 1–4.

GARTER STITCH

You've learned how to knit a stitch. If you keep knitting all of your stitches in every row you will produce the Garter stitch. This stitch makes a very sturdy, bumpy, ridge-like pattern. If you are following a pattern and it says, "Work in Garter stitch," that simply means you will knit all stitches in every row. If you want to know how many rows you have created in your project, just count the horizontal ridges (see photo above). Each ridge is equal to two rows, so if you counted twelve ridges, your project is twenty-four rows long. The good news? All of the projects in this lesson use Garter stitch, so give one a try!

CHEEP TRICKS

Always try to finish a row in your knitting before putting down your project. If for some reason you have to put down your work in the middle of a row, make sure that when you come back to it you pick up the needle with the yarn ball attached in your right hand (left hand if you're a southpaw).

ADDING A NEW BALL OF YARN

When you run out of one ball of yarn, you'll simply add a new ball. It's best to join the new ball at the beginning of a row. To join the yarn, leave at least a 6" tail from the existing yarn and loosely tie the new yarn to it, leaving another 6" tail. Later, when your project is finished, you can untie the knot and weave both ends into the piece.

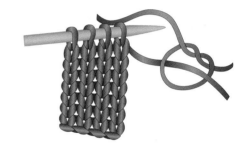

ADDING FRINGE

If you want to up the "wow" factor on a scarf or shawl, fringe can be used to dramatic effect. Go with longer fringe for a retro '70s vibe or give your project youthful kick with shorter fringe—you can even choose contrasting colors to the main garment! Fringe is a truly versatile embellishment, and also incredibly easy to do. Here's how:

1. Cut yarn into as many pieces and to whatever length is called for in the pattern.
2. Using two pieces of yarn, fold in half.
3. Insert crochet hook through stitch along bottom edge of garment where you wish to add fringe.
4. Place folded pieces of yarn on hook and pull through stitch, making a loop.
5. Now push yarn ends through loop and pull tightly. Repeat across remaining stitches.

END IT ALL: BINDING OFF

To finish a project you must bind off, or—to put it literally—get the stitches off the needle without having them unravel. Here is how to bind off:

1. Loosely knit the first and second stitches in a row. Insert the left-hand needle into the first stitch you knitted and lift that stitch over the second stitch and off the needle. You will have one stitch remaining on the needle.
2. Knit the next stitch so you again have two stitches on the right-hand needle and lift the first stitch over the one you have just knitted.
3. Repeat step 2 until there is only one stitch left on the left-hand needle.
4. To secure the final stitch, or fasten off, cut the yarn from the ball, leaving a 4–6" tail. Pull the tail through the last stitch and pull it tight. With the remaining tail, you will weave in the yarn ends as described in "Weaving in Yarn Ends," below.

WEAVING IN YARN ENDS

When you finish a project, you may have a bunch of loose, dangling yarn tails hanging from the piece. But resist the urge to cut them off—we'll show you how to hide them instead, which keeps your garment secure. Thread a finishing needle with the yarn end. With the wrong side of your piece facing up, weave the needle through several stitches in the back of the work. Clip any remaining ends close to the project. Check your work from the front side to be sure no yarn ends are showing through.

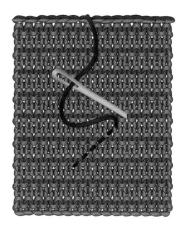

You Go, Girl! Scarf

Scarf

Working with both yarns held together, cast on 24 stitches.

1. Work in Garter stitch (Knit every row).
2. When piece measures 50" from beginning, bind off.

Fringe

1. Cut 36 pieces of each yarn, all 16" long.
2. Using 2 pieces of each yarn, fold in half.
3. Insert crochet hook through stitch along bottom edge of scarf where you wish to add fringe.
4. Place folded pieces of yarn on hook and pull through stitch, making a loop.
5. Now push yarn ends through loop and pull tightly. Repeat across remaining stitches.
6. Repeat steps for opposite edge of scarf.

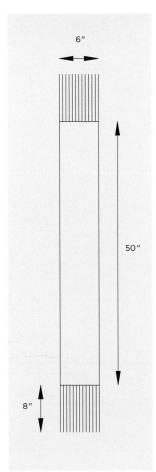

6"

50"

8"

CHICK FEED

This is a very manageable project for a beginner. We've added a little sizzle with a metallic strand, and you can up the oomph factor by adding fringe if you like. Don't be surprised if you see your knitting vastly improve from when you start working on this scarf to when you finish.

The Envelope Bag

Completed Measurements

Approximately 11" x 13" before felting

Approximately 8" x 3" after felting

Materials

~ 100 yd/92 m worsted weight wool

~ 100 yd/92 m novelty yarn

~ 50 yd/46 m novelty yarn

~ Size US 15 needles

~ Finishing needle

~ Large sewing needle

~ Button

*Sample was knitted using Plymouth Galway
(3.5 oz/100 g, 210 yd/192 m per ball;
100% wool) in Celadon Green; Plymouth
Athena (1.75 oz/50 g, 77 yd/71 m per ball;
51% cotton, 44% nylon, 5% rayon) in #54;
and Plymouth Eros (1.75 oz/50 g, 165 yd/
150 m per ball; 100% nylon) in #715.*

Bag

Using wool and main novelty yarn held together, cast on 30 stitches

1. Knit every row until piece measures 13".

2. Bind off.

3. Fold bottom third up, like an envelope, and whipstitch sides together.

4. Felt the bag (see Lesson 5, "Take it Away," page 54, for felting instructions).

Finishing

Note before finishing: Refer to Lesson 22, "Getting It All Together" (page 147), for instructions on various finishing techniques.

1. Using the novelty yarn and a sewing needle, whipstitch along front of opening and top edge of flap to create a decorative edge.

2. Using novelty yarn, make a loop at center of top flap to loop over button.

3. Sew on button.

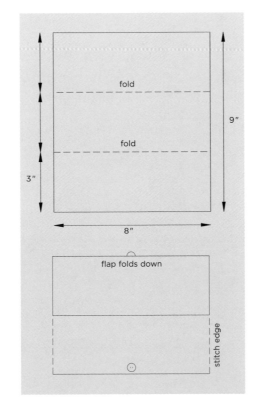

CHICK FEED

Our colorful little bag is just the right size to use as an eyeglass case, a makeup case, or even an evening clutch—it fits right in the palm of your hand! When you've finished knitting this bag, one option is to felt it, which melts away most minor imperfections.

PURLS ARE A GIRL'S BEST FRIEND

~~~~~~

PURL STITCH

The Purl stitch is actually the reverse of the Knit stitch. Every time you create a Knit stitch it forms a little V shape. If you turn your work over and look at the back, you've also created a little bump, or "purl." To make those purls appear on the right side of the fabric, we bring the yarn to the front of our work and insert the needle into the front of the stitch. Just mastering these techniques of Knit and Purl opens you up to endless stitch combinations and possibilities.

Here's how it's done:

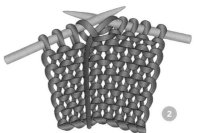

1. Hold the needle with your cast-on stitches in your left hand, with the yarn held in front. Insert the right-hand needle in the first stitch from back to front. Wrap the yarn around the right-hand needle counter-clockwise; the yarn now will be between both needles.

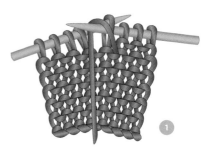

2. Bring the right-hand needle backward through the stitch on the left-hand needle, catching the yarn and pulling it backward through the stitch on the left-hand needle.

3. Slip the stitch off the left-hand needle, leaving a new stitch on the right-hand needle.

4 Repeat these steps until all the newly formed stitches are on the right-hand needle.

5 Start the next row by moving the needle that is holding the stitches to your left hand and the empty needle to your right hand. Repeat steps 1–4.

Purl Stitch for Southpaws

1 Hold the needle with your cast-on stitches in your right hand, with the yarn held in front. Insert the left-hand needle in the first stitch from back to front. Wrap the yarn around the left-hand needle clockwise. The yarn now will be between both needles.

2 Bring the left-hand needle backward through the stitch on the right-hand needle, catching the yarn and pulling it backward through the stitch on the right-hand needle.

3 Slip the stitch off the right-hand needle, leaving a new stitch on the left-hand needle.

4 Repeat these steps until all the newly formed stitches are on the left-hand needle.

5 Start the next row by moving the needle that is holding the stitches to your right hand and the empty needle to your left hand. Repeat steps 1–4.

How Should the Stitches Look?

Telling the difference between a Knit and a Purl stitch allows you to identify what you are doing and whether you may have made a mistake along the way.

Knit Stitch ~ Smooth and looks like a V.

Purl Stitch ~ Looks like a little bump or a little pearl.

STOCKINETTE STITCH

This stitch is a combination of knitting one row then purling one row, and alternating these two rows throughout your project. Stockinette is a very common stitch. Look in your closet at your T-shirts, socks, and sweaters. Most ready-to-wear knitted garments use this stitch. It knits up very smoothly on the Knit side (right side) and very bumpy on the Purl side (wrong side). This is how a Stockinette stitch pattern is written:

~ Row 1 Knit across row.

~ Row 2 Purl across row.

~ Repeat Rows 1 and 2.

CHEEP TRICKS

Stockinette stitch has a tendency to roll at the edges. If you are knitting a scarf in Stockinette stitch, it is usually a good idea to trim the scarf with a border or edge stitch to keep it from rolling. Our Dirty-Girl Washcloth in Stockinette stitch trimmed with Garter stitch (above left) is a perfect example. When Stockinette stitch is used in a sweater or garment, the side seams control the curl and allow it to stay flat.

Note

The **right side** of your garment is the side that will be seen, just like the right side of a piece of printed material. The **wrong side** is the back side of the fabric that will not be seen.

REVERSE STOCKINETTE STITCH

Reverse Stockinette stitch (above center) is the same as Stockinette stitch: The only difference is that the Purl side (bumpy side) is the right side and the Knit side (smooth side) is the wrong side.

BASKET WEAVE STITCH

This is a great stitch for its interesting texture, as it resembles the weave of a basket (above right). This stitch looks the same on both sides and is great for sweaters, scarves, and men's garments. The Basket Weave stitch can be written like this:

~ Rows 1–4 Knit 4, Purl 4. Repeat across row.
~ Rows 5–8 Purl 4, Knit 4. Repeat across row.
~ Repeat Rows 1–8.

Dirty-Girl Washcloths

Garter Stitch Washcloth

Using Peach yarn, cast on 50 sts

1. Work in Garter st (Knit every row) until almost out of yarn.
2. Bind off loosely.
3. Weave in all yarn ends.

Stockinette Stitch with Garter Stitch Edge Washcloth

Using Magenta yarn, cast on 50 sts

1. Knit 5 rows.
2. K5, P40, Knit last 5 sts.
3. Knit.
4. Repeat Rows 2 and 3 for 40 rows.
5. Knit 5 rows.
6. Bind off loosely.
7. Weave in all yarn ends.

Basket Weave Washcloth

Using Purple yarn, cast on 50 sts

1. Work Rows 1–10 of Basket Weave Pattern Stitch Pattern for approximately 9".
2. Bind off loosely in st pattern.
3. Weave in all yarn ends.

CHEEP TRICKS

Always bind off in the established stitch pattern. For example, if you are working in a K5, P5 stitch pattern, you will bind off that way as well.

FLY THE COOP!

Use any new stitch pattern you wish to design your own washcloths.

Beginner

Completed Measurements
Approximately 10" x 10"

Materials
~ 250 yd/228 m heavy worsted weight cotton or cotton blend yarn
~ Size US 6 needles
~ Finishing needle

Abbreviation Key
K	Knit
P	Purl
st(s)	stitch(es)

Samples were knitted in Reynolds, Blossom (1.75 oz/50 g, 82 yd/75 m per ball, 50% acrylic, 40% viscose, 10% cotton) in Peach, Magenta, and Purple.

Stitch Guide:
Basket Weave Stitch Pattern
~ Rows 1–5 *Knit 5, Purl 5*. Repeat from * to * across row.
~ Rows 6–10 *Purl 5, Knit 5*. Repeat from * to * across row.

CHICK FEED

These small projects will allow you to try your hand at the interesting new stitches we've introduced in this lesson. The washcloths work up quickly and make a great on-the-go, portable project. They are the perfect hostess or housewarming gift; make all three in coordinating colors, add a bar of your favorite soap, and tie with a ribbon!

Boyfriend Basket Weave Scarf

Completed Measurements
Approximately 6 ¹/₂" x 50"

Materials
~ 219 yd/200 m chunky weight yarn
~ Size US 6 needles
~ Finishing needle

Abbreviation Key
st(s)   stitch(es)

*Sample was knitted in Adrienne Vittadini,
Donata (1.75 oz/50 g, 73 yd/68 m per ball;
70% alpaca, 30% acrylic) in Brown.*

Stitch Guide:
Basket Weave Stitch Pattern
~ Rows 1–4 *Knit 4, Purl 4*. Repeat
  from * to * across row.
~ Rows 5–8 *Purl 4, Knit 4*. Repeat
  from * to * across row.
~ Repeat Rows 1–8.

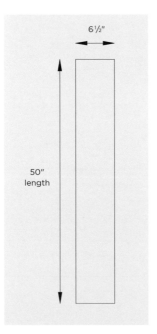

6½"

50"
length

Scarf

Cast on 32 sts

1. Work Rows 1–8 of Basket Weave Stitch
   Pattern until scarf measures approximately
   50", or desired length.
2. Bind off in st pattern.
3. Weave in all yarn ends.

CHEEP TRICKS

Make this for your boyfriend, but
chances are you'll like it so much
you'll want to keep it for yourself!
Men's garments are usually knitted on
small needles, so you'll notice the
plushness and bounce when knitting
this item. For example, we selected a
chunky weight yarn, which called for a
size 10 needle on the yarn label. Since
we wanted the fabric to be thick and
tightly knit, we took it all the way
down to a size 6 needle.

Artisan Belt

Belt

Cast on 9 sts

1. Knit first 6 sts, bring yarn forward, then slip last 3 sts as if to Purl (refer to "Slipping Stitches" below for help).
2. Repeat Row 2 until desired length.
3. Bind off.
4. Weave in all yarn ends.
5. Attach belt buckle of your choice to complete belt.

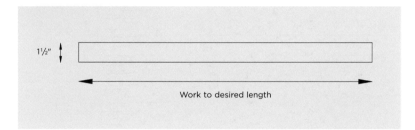

1½" ↕

Work to desired length

Slipping Stitches

Occasionally a pattern will instruct you to slip a stitch. This means that you are slipping the stitches from the left-hand needle to the right-hand needle without knitting them. Slipped stitches are often used to make a cleaner edge on a knitted project or to help keep edges from rolling. In the Artisan Belt project we will be using slipped stitches to make rolled edges on the sides of a belt.

   Patterns will usually state whether you should slip as if to Purl or slip as if to Knit. This just means that you will insert the right-hand needle as if you are going to Knit or as if you are going to Purl and slide the stitch over to the right-hand needle without knitting or purling it.

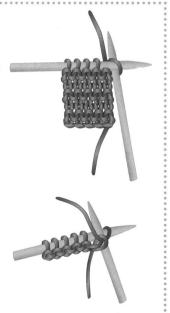

Advanced Beginner

Completed Measurements

~ 1 ½" wide by desired length

~ For tie belt, measure waist and add 6"

~ For buckle belt, measure waist and add 2"

~ Don't make the belt too long, as it tends to stretch through wear.

Materials

~ 75 yd/69 m worsted weight yarn

~ Size US 4 needles

~ Finishing needle

Sample belt was knitted in Judy & Co. Corde yarn (3.5 oz/100 g, 100 yd/91 m per ball; 100% rayon with a cotton core,) in Cappuccino

Abbreviation Key

st(s)   stitch(es)

CHICK FEED

Our Artisan Belt may be knitted using just about any type of yarn. What makes this belt unique is that you will be making a rolled edge just by slipping a few stitches! This is a great, quick gift idea.

GIVE ME MORE

INCREASING

There are times when you need to add stitches to your knitted piece to make it wider, such as in a sleeve. This is called increasing. There are several ways to increase stitches on your needle. We are going to show you our two favorites, the Make 1 Method and the Knit in Front and Back Method. They seem to do the trick in most situations.

Make 1 Increase (m 1), aka the Bar Method

The Make 1 invisible increase is the least visible kind of increasing method and as such can be used in the majority of your projects. It is made by picking up the horizontal line, or "bar," between two stitches and then knitting the bar. You are essentially creating a stitch from the knitted fabric where there wasn't one before.

Don't be shy, give it a try! Using the left-hand needle, pick up the horizontal bar from back to front (1) and Knit as if it was a stitch (2) (it will feel a little tight to knit). This method may be used on a Knit row or a Purl row. If you are on a Purl row you will pick up the bar in the same manner, but you will then Purl that stitch.

CHEEP TRICKS

If your increase feels very easy to knit (in other words, not a little bit tight), make sure to check that you have picked up your stitch the right way, from the back. Picking up the stitch from the front will leave a hole in your knitting.

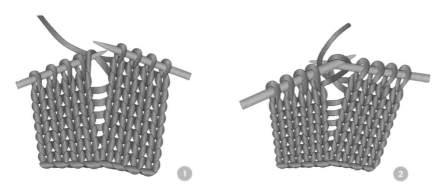

Knit in Front and Back Increase (inc 1 st, or Kfb)

This type of increase creates a small bar that is visible on the right side of the fabric. It is very easy to make but not often used in more advanced patterns because it doesn't give as much of a polished look as the Make 1 increase.

Here's how it's done: Insert the needle into the next stitch, Knit that stitch but do not take the stitch off the needle (1). Now insert the needle into the back of that same stitch and Knit this stitch again (2). This will create another stitch.

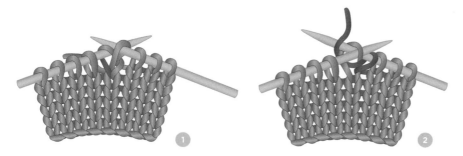

Urban Wrap

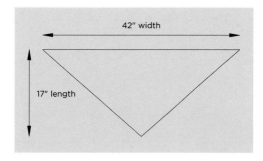

42" width

17" length

Size
One size fits most

Completed Measurements
42" wide x 17" long at the point (not including fringe)

Materials
~ 200 yd/183 m chunky mohair yarn
~ Size US 15 needles
~ Size J/6.0 mm crochet hook for fringe
~ Finishing needle

Sample was knitted in Be Sweet, Brushed Mohair (1.75 oz/50 g, 110 yd/100 m per ball; 100% baby mohair) in Charcoal.

Abbreviation Key
K	Knit
P	Purl
st(s)	stitch(es)

Gauge
7 sts and 12 rows to 4" over Stockinette stitch (K 1 row, P 1 row) on size 15 needles, or size needed to obtain gauge

Stitch Guide: Make 1 Increase (m 1)

Pick up the horizontal bar between two stitches by inserting the left-hand needle from back to front and then Knit or Purl (depending on the row) this stitch.

Wrap

Cast on 3 sts

~ Row 1 K1, m 1, Knit remaining sts across row—this is the right side.

~ Row 2 P1, m 1, Purl remaining sts across row—this is the wrong side.

~ Repeat Rows 1 and 2 until there are 60 sts on needle. End with a wrong side row.

Next Section

~ Row 1 K1, m 1, Knit across to last st, m 1, Knit last st.

~ Row 2 P1, m 1, Purl across to last st, m 1, Purl last st.

~ Repeat Rows 1 and 2 until there are 150 sts on needle.

~ Bind off very loosely. (You need to bind off loosely to allow the top edge of the wrap to stretch to the right proportion.)

Fringe

1. Cut 108 pieces of yarn, each 16" long.

2. Using 2 pieces of yarn, fold in half.

3. Insert crochet hook through stitch where you'd like to add fringe along right edge of wrap.

4. Place folded pieces of yarn on hook and pull through stitch, making a loop.

5. Push ends through loop and pull tightly. Repeat across remaining sts.

6. Repeat above steps for opposite edge of wrap.

FLY THE COOP!
For a more luxurious look, take a short-haired, soft-bristled brush and brush the mohair lightly, until it fluffs.

CHICK FEED
Wrap yourself in a little luxury! In this project you will get to practice knitting, purling, increasing, and making fringe. We knitted this project using mohair because of its light, airy feel and warmth. An added bonus: Mohair is usually knitted on larger needles, so it's a faster knit project!

TAKE IT AWAY

~~~~~~

DECREASING

Decreasing is the process of shaping your knitting by making it narrower, which means eliminating a stitch or stitches. The most commonly used decreases for beginners are Knit 2 Together or Purl 2 Together, depending on what row you are on. These decreases may be used in most knitting projects and are very simple to learn.

Later in this chapter, after you've mastered the art of decreasing your stitches, we'll teach you how to make your entire project smaller by a shrinking process called "felting." Felting is a fun and easy way to transform the look and feel of your finished project into a denser, smoother finish.

Decreasing on a Knit Row: Knit 2 Together (K2tog)

Knit through two stitches at the same time. This will make one Knit stitch out of two stitches.

Here's how it's done:

1. Insert right needle into next two stitches at the same time.
2. Wrap yarn counterclockwise around right needle.
3. Pull up a loop through both stitches.
4. Slide stitches from left needle.
5. New stitch should now be on your right needle—one decrease made.

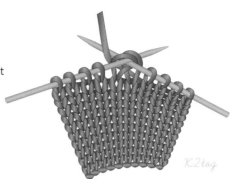

K2tog

Decreasing on a Purl Row: Purl 2 Together (P2tog)

Purl through two stitches at the same time. This will make one Purl stitch out of two stitches.

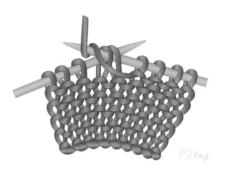

P2tog

FACTS ABOUT FELTING

Have you ever shrunk a wool sweater by accident? Well, felting is the process of purposely shrinking wool using hot or warm water and agitation. This irreversible process causes the wool hairs to tangle and bind together to form a very thick, durable fabric. Does the type of yarn you select matter? Yes! You need to choose a yarn that is 100% wool—suitable for felting. Some Merino wools have been treated so they will not felt. Most wool blends also will not felt. Your local yarn shop can help you select wools that are appropriate for this process.

We are often asked, "I've spent all this time knitting; why would I want to felt something?" What is so spectacular about felting is that you end up with a very rich, dense material, perfect for knitted bags, hats, slippers, and needle cases. Felting truly turns knitting from a hobby into an art form. You take a ball of yarn and knit it into this loose shape, and then the felting process totally changes the feel of the yarn, making it more pliable. The knit fabric can be shaped while still wet and even cut without it unraveling or fraying.

CHEEP TRICKS

When you are increasing and decreasing, you must stay in the stitch pattern. Look at the stitch you are working and determine if it is a Knit stitch or Purl stitch (explained in Lesson 2, "The Chicks' Knitting Crash Course," page 29). This will help you decide which stitch you need to work next to keep your pattern consistent.

Step-by-Step Felting Instructions

To felt a project you will need:

- A washing machine with good agitation
- A zippered pillow protector (a lingerie bag is not suitable to protect your washer from excess lint and fiber)
- An old pair of jeans or khakis
- A few large towels

CHEEP TRICKS

You'll need to experiment to get the look you want. Every washing machine felts differently, and each item you felt may require a different amount of felting time. . . . Felting is an art, not a science!

1. Be prepared to be near your washing machine during the felting process. Set the washer to the smallest load and hottest water settings. Add a small amount of laundry soap. Place the item to be felted inside a pillow protector, and place it in the washing machine. Add a pair of jeans or khakis to help with the agitation process.

2. Check the washer after 5 minutes; the wool will absorb the water and actually seem to get looser.

3. Check the washer after 8–10 minutes. You should notice the stitches becoming "fuzzier" and beginning to blur together.

4. Check again every 3–5 minutes. Do NOT allow the machine to go through the rinse or spin cycle. When the felting item appears to be the correct size (you should no longer be able to see the stitches, and the fabric will feel very thick), remove it from the washer and hand rinse in cold water.

5. Gently squeeze out the excess water (do not wring). Wrap the item in towels to remove as much water as possible. Do NOT put your project in the dryer.

6. After you have felted a project and you remove it from the washing machine, think of it as a ball of clay. You may need to stretch and shape it a bit to achieve just the right look. Don't be afraid to really give it a tug or pull—it is quite strong. When felting tote bags, we always try to find an empty box to use as a mold. Allow the item to air-dry overnight.

> **Don't miss a chance to get felted!**
>
> Be sure to try all the felted projects in this book. Check out the Envelope Bag on page 39, the Bohemian Felted Hobo Bag on page 77, and the Bohemian Felted Needle Case on page 79.

The Scoop Bag

CHICK FEED

Here's "the scoop" on this bag: It's an easy-to-knit felted shoulder bag that will tuck under your arm and add a little sophistication to your outfit. It stands alone, or you may opt to add the flower embellishments. Try adding these flowers to just about anything: hats, sweaters, other bags, etc. . . . Let your creativity guide you!

Completed Measurements

Approximately 21" x 14" before felting
Approximately 17" x 11" after felting

Materials

~276 yd/252 m heavy worsted weight
  yarn in yellow-green
~100 yd/91 m heavy worsted weight
  yarn in magenta for flowers
~50 yd/46 m novelty ribbon yarn
  for flowers
~Size US 13 needles
~Two 3" metal rings
~Sewing needle
~Sewing thread
~Finishing needle
~Beads (optional)

Abbreviation Key

beg	beginning
dec	decrease
inc	increase
K	Knit
K2tog	Knit 2 stitches together
m 1	Make 1 (inc)
P	Purl
sl	slip stitch
st(s)	stitch(es)
St st	Stockinette stitch
yo	yarn over

*Sample was knitted in Manos del Uruguay
(3.5 oz/100 g, 138 yd/126 m per ball; 100%
wool) in Citric and Art yarn Silk Ribbon (.88 oz/
25 g, 128 yd/117 m; 100% silk) in Magenta.*

Gauge

12 sts and 16 rows to 4" over St st (K 1 row, P 1 row) on size 13 needles, or size needed to obtain gauge

Stitch Guide:
Make 1 Increase (m 1)

The increase in this pattern is done by picking up the horizontal bar between 2 stitches. You will be using this method for both the Knit row and Purl row.
~Knit 1, Make 1 stitch, Knit across to last stitch, Make 1 stitch, Knit last stitch—this is the right side.
~Purl 1, Make 1 stitch, Purl across to last stitch, Make 1 stitch, Purl last stitch—this is the wrong side.

Note

When using a novelty yarn, make the flowers the same way but do NOT felt them. Using different yarn gives dimension and texture to your flowers, so experiment and have fun with them.

Bag (make 2)

Cast on 33 sts

Work in St st.

~ Rows 1–39 m 1 at beg and end of every 3 rows 13 times.

~ Row 40 Work 20 sts, attach a new ball of yarn. With new yarn bind off center 19 sts, complete the row. You now will be working both sides of the bag at the same time, each side using its own ball of yarn. The bound-off section will be referred to as the Bag Opening for the remainder of this pattern.

~ Row 41 Dec 1 st (K2tog) at beg and end of Bag Opening.

~ Row 42 m 1 st at beg and end of row, dec 1 st at beg and end of Bag Opening.

~ Rows 43–44 Dec 1 st at beg and end of Bag Opening.

~ Row 45 m 1 st at beg and end of row, and dec 1 st at beg and end of Bag Opening.

~ Rows 46–47 Dec 1 st at beg and end of Bag Opening.

~ Row 48 m 1 st at beg and end of row, dec 1 st at beg and end of Bag Opening.

~ Rows 49–50 Dec 1 st at beg and of Bag Opening.

~ Row 51 m 1 st at beg and end of row, dec 1 st at beg and end of Bag Opening.

~ Rows 52–54 Dec 1 st at beg and end of Bag Opening.

~ Rows 55–60 Continue working in St st.

~ Bind off.

~ Whipstitch front and back of bag together (see page 152).

~ Felt bag (both bag and strap may be felted together).

Strap

Cast on 15 sts

1. Work in St st until piece measures 20" from beg.

2. Bind off.

3. Felt strap (both bag and strap may be felted together).

Finishing

1. When the bag is completely dry after felting, you may line it with a fabric of your choice, if you desire.

2. Place rings at either side of bag, folding approximately 1" of strap and bag over rings, and sew in place using whipstitch (see page 152).

3. Attach flowers (see "Flowers" below for flower instructions).

4. Embellish flowers with beads (optional).

Flowers

Cast on 30 sts

~ Row 1 Knit.

~ Row 2 K1, *yo, K1*. Repeat from * to * across to end. Knit last st. Refer to Lesson 13, "Over the Yarn We Go!" (page 103), for yarn over instructions.

~ Repeat Rows 1 and 2 another 2 times.

~ Bind off loosely in st pattern and felt finished flowers.

~ When dry, spiral each piece to form the flowers; if you want smaller flowers, just cut each piece in half before spiraling. Attach to bag by sewing them on with a sewing needle and thread.

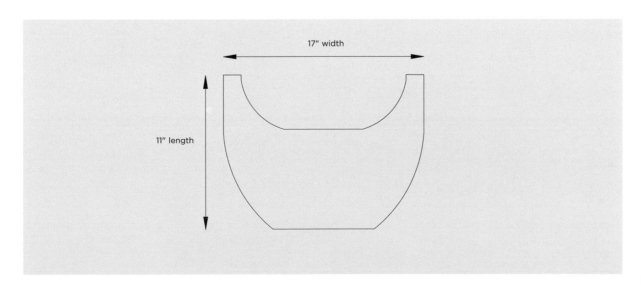

TAKE A TEST DRIVE

~~~~~~

Up to this point it wasn't really important if you made a test swatch. We wanted you to get a taste for knitting and just relax and enjoy the process. Now we are stepping it up a notch. The projects going forward will require that you knit a test swatch before you begin. This lesson explains why making a test swatch is so important.

WHAT IS A TEST SWATCH?

When buying a car, you usually take it out for a test drive. You check that it is the right fit for you; that it's comfortable; that it serves your needs; and, most of all, that it looks good! A test swatch is like a test drive for your knitting. It is a sample swatch knitted using the yarn and needles you plan to use for a project. You'll check that the yarn is just the right fit for the pattern; that it feels good; that it serves your needs; and, most of all, that it looks good!

How to Make a Test Swatch

1. Using your selected yarn and suggested needle size noted in the pattern, knit a 5″ x 5″ test swatch. The pattern will tell you which stitch to use.

2. To figure out how many stitches to cast on, start by using the number of stitches noted in the pattern's gauge and adding 10. For example, the pattern may state: "20 stitches and 26 rows to 4″ over Stockinette stitch on size 8 needles." You will make a test swatch of approximately 30 stitches in Stockinette stitch using size 8 needles.

3. Lay the test swatch on a flat surface.

4. Using a ruler, count how many stitches and how many rows are in 4″. This will tell you your gauge.

I'VE MADE A TEST SWATCH, NOW WHAT?

I have the right number of stitches to match the gauge.
Go ahead and begin your project.

Help, I have too many stitches!
If you have too many stitches, your gauge is too tight; try making the swatch again using larger needles.

Help, I don't have enough stitches!
If you have too few stitches, your gauge is too loose; try making the swatch again using smaller needles.

Help, my stitches are uneven!
Most likely you need to work on maintaining even tension in your knitting. Keep practicing, and your tension will improve.

Project Ideas!

Don't throw away your gauge swatches! Here are two great ideas for putting those swatches to good use:

1. Knitting Scrapbook
   Swatches can be excellent reference tools for future projects. For this reason, many knitters keep a "knitting scrapbook." It usually includes the gauge swatch, pattern, notes made while knitting, and even a photo of the person wearing the completed garment.

2. Swatch Blanket
   Save your gauge swatches, and when you've stashed enough of them, knit them together into a blanket and donate it to charity!

ANATOMY OF A GARMENT

UNDERSTANDING GARMENT CONSTRUCTION

There are several ways to make a sweater, including bottom-up, top-down, and flat-panel construction. The bottom-up method begins at the lower edge of the garment and requires working the front and back as one piece. The sleeves are worked separately, and then all the pieces are joined at the same time; the yoke (the fitted portion at the neck and shoulders) is worked as one piece. This method is usually considered a more advanced type of garment construction. The biggest advantage to the bottom-up method is that it requires very little finishing, as there are few or no seams to sew. Top-down construction is appealing for the same reason but works the process in reverse. The garment begins at the neck, and the front and back are worked in one piece. Stitches are skipped for the sleeve openings, then resumed for the front and back, all done in one piece down to the waist. The most common method is known as flat-panel construction. That simply means panels are constructed individually in flat-panel pieces. The back, front, and sleeves are knitted separately and then sewn together. Take a look at some of the store-bought sweaters in your closet, which were most likely made using this method.

In the following project we will walk you step by step through the process of making a simple shell. You will learn how to make a garment that fits, map out your pattern, and put those pieces together.

SWEATER STICKER SHOCK

Years ago, knitting clothes for warmth was a necessity. Today with retailing giants able to sell sweaters for low prices—some as low as $20—knitting isn't a necessity. What it has turned into is a great hobby with yarns that appeal to many taste levels and wallets. Most of the smaller projects you have knitted so far only required a few balls of yarn; but as you begin to get into larger projects, such as garments, the projects will require quite a bit more yarn. The yarn to knit sweaters can be rather pricey and lead to a lot of hesitation to make the leap into such a big (and costly) project. We always suggest that you purchase the best yarn you can afford. After all, you are going to spend many hours laboring over a project; plus, part of the enjoyment of knitting is the tactile feel of the yarn and how beautiful the garment is when it is completed. The difference between an acrylic craft yarn and a hand-dyed luxury natural fiber is unbelievable. Try using the right type of yarn for a given project. To make a small purse, for example, you may need to choose durable wool rather than a delicate ribbon yarn. Along those lines, to knit a sweater, it may be a better choice to use hand-dyed wool or soft cotton rather than a craft yarn.

Knittin' Pretty Simple Shell

Advanced Beginner

Sizes

It's time to pick the size of the garment you want to knit. Pull out a great-fitting sweater from your closet (it can be store-bought). Lay it on a flat surface and measure it across just under the arms. Double that number and that will be the size you will use. For example, if your sweater measures 18" across, 36" is the size you should go with. Some patterns will size their garments with ease measurements built in, claiming they will fit sizes 32, 34, 36, etc, but always look for the *finished* measurement. That is the true size of the garment when knitted, assuming your gauge is accurate, of course!

Petite (Small, Medium, Large, X-Large)

Completed Chest Measurements
32 (34, 36, 38, 40)"

Materials
- ~450 (450, 450, 600, 600) yd/411 (411, 411, 548, 548) m heavy worsted weight yarn
- ~Size US 9 needles
- ~Size J/6.0 mm crochet hook for crocheted neckline and armholes
- ~Finishing needle

Abbreviation Key

beg	beginning
dec	decrease
K	knit
K2tog	Knit 2 stitches together
st(s)	stitch(es)

Sample was knitted in Collinette Giotto (3.5 oz/ 100 g, 154 yd/140 m per hank; 50% cotton, 40% rayon, 10 % nylon) in Marble.

Gauge

18 sts and 32 rows to 4" over Garter st (Knit every row) on size 9 needles, or size needed to obtain gauge

Back

Garments usually start with the Back. This is usually the largest piece and, in this case, the easiest. After you finish the Back of this project, more than half of your garment will be complete!

Cast on 72 (76, 82, 86, 90) sts

1. Work in Garter st (Knit every row) until piece measures 13" from beg.
2. Begin armhole shaping as follows: bind off 3 (4, 5, 5, 6) sts at beg of next 2 rows.

CHICK FEED

Welcome to your first knitted garment. We have set up this project as a tutorial to guide you through each step necessary to complete this shell. The information we are providing in this project is not usually found in a pattern, but it is information you would learn if you were sitting in a yarn shop taking a class. Use this shell pattern as a stepping stone to move from knitting simple projects to knitting garments.

The Chicks' Knitting Shorthand

It's time to learn Knitting Shorthand and how to organize your pattern information to work through your project.

Why do I have to learn Knitting Shorthand?

As you advance as a knitter, the difficulty of your projects will too. We are providing you with the tools to be able to work through the most complex stitches and garments without missing a stitch. Just as a child must learn numbers before being able to write math problems, knitters have to become comfortable with reading a pattern and making a few projects before moving on to more advanced projects. Now you will have several things to remember while working rows. Instead of making yourself crazy trying to keep your row/decrease information in your head, Knitting Shorthand is a note system that will allow you to continue knitting as comfortably as before, even on more complex projects.

What Is Knitting Shorthand?

Take a look at the remainder of the Back of this project, step 3 in particular: "Dec 1 st (K2tog) at beg and end of every other row, 3 (3, 4, 5, 5) times." In the case of the smallest size, it means that you will be decreasing at the beginning and end of every other row over a total of 6 rows. Do you think we remember all that information in our heads while knitting? We don't. We simply write out the rows like this:

~ Row 1 Knit.

~ Row 2 Dec 1 st at beg and end of row.

~ Row 3 Knit.

~ Row 4 Dec 1 st at beg and end of row.

~ Row 5 Knit.

~ Row 6 Dec 1 st at beg and end of row.

After you complete a row, check it off. You can set this project down, come back to it anytime, look at your notes, and know exactly where to pick up and work!

---

3. Dec 1 st (K2tog) at beg and end of every other row 3 (3, 4, 5, 5) times.
4 Work in Garter st until piece measures 21 (21, 21, 22, 22)″ from beg.
5. Bind off loosely.

Front

Cast on 72 (76, 82, 86, 90) sts

1. Work in Garter st until piece measures 13″ from beg.
2. Begin armhole shaping as follows: bind off 3 (4, 5, 5, 6) at beg of next 2 rows.
3. Dec 1 st at beg and end of every other row 3 (3, 4, 5, 5) times.
4. Work in Garter st until piece measures 19 (19, 19, 20, 20)″ from beg.

Begin neck shaping as follows: Work 22 (22, 23, 24, 25) sts, attach a new ball of yarn. With new yarn bind off center 16 (18, 18, 18, 18) sts, complete the row (see page 67). You now will be working both sides of the shoulders at the same time, each side using its own ball of yarn.

Binding Off in the Middle of a Row

This is the point in this garment where you will have to bind off in the middle of the row to properly shape the neck. We broke this down into steps to help make this process painless:

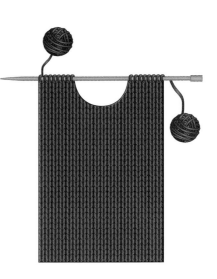

1. Work the stitches to the point where you will need to bind off.
2. Add a new ball of yarn (refer to Lesson 9, "Horse of a Different Color," page 72).
3. Drop the old yarn and bind off the middle stitches with the new yarn.
4. Continue working the row with the new yarn.
5. You now will be working both sides of the shoulders at the same time, each side using its own ball of yarn.
6. Dec 1 st at each neck edge every other row 6 times. Use your Knitting Shorthand to write this down, and check off each row after you finish it.
7. Continue working in Garter st until piece measures same as Back.
8. Bind off loosely.

Finishing

Note before finishing: Refer to Lesson 22, "Getting It All Together" (page 147), for instructions on various finishing techniques.

1. Sew shoulder seams together using horizontal-to-horizontal mattress stitch.
2. Sew side seams using vertical-to-vertical mattress stitch.
3. Single crochet around neckline and armholes if desired.
4. Weave in all yarn ends.

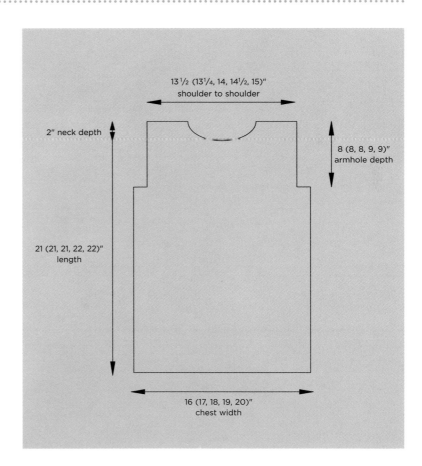

13 1/2 (13 1/4, 14, 14 1/2, 15)"
shoulder to shoulder

2" neck depth

8 (8, 8, 9, 9)"
armhole depth

21 (21, 21, 22, 22)"
length

16 (17, 18, 19, 20)"
chest width

NOTHING UP OUR SLEEVES

ADDING SLEEVES

In the last lesson you learned step-by-step how to knit a simple shell. We provided a lot of extra information regarding Knitting Shorthand in order to make knitting your first garment easy. Our Five Below Sweater takes it a step further by adding sleeves. We'll walk you through the steps of sleeve shaping by showing you how to map out your pattern on paper so you don't lose track of your progress.

Five Below Sweater

CHICK FEED
This is truly a project that can be knitted in little more than a weekend! We used a super chunky weight yarn and large needles to make it go fast—and provide a little of that instant gratification we all appreciate. Knit it this weekend and you'll be wearing it on the ski slopes at the first snowfall!

Back

Cast on 36 (38, 40, 44, 46) sts

1. Work in St st until piece measures 14 (14, 14, 15, 15)" from beg.
2. Begin armhole shaping as follows: bind off 2 (2, 3, 3, 3) sts at beg of next 2 rows.
3. Dec 1 st (K2tog) at beg and end of every other row 1 (2, 2, 2, 2) times. Use your Knitting Shorthand (see page 66) to keep track of the steps.
4. Continue working in St st until piece measures 22 (22, 22, 24, 24)" from beg.
5. Bind off remaining sts.

Front

Cast on 36 (38, 40, 44, 46) sts

1. Work in St st until piece measures 14 (14, 14, 15, 15)" from beg.
2. Begin armhole shaping as follows: bind off 2 (2, 3, 3, 3) sts at beg of next 2 rows.
3. Dec 1 st at beg and end of every other row 1 (2, 2, 2, 2) times.
4. Work in St st for one more inch, then begin neck shaping.
5. Begin neck shaping as follows: Work 15 (15, 15, 17, 18) sts, attach a new ball of yarn. With new yarn, work remaining sts. You now will be working both sides of the shoulders at the same time, each side using its own ball of yarn.
6. Dec 1 st at each neck edge every 2nd row 4 (4, 5, 8, 8) times. Then dec 1 st at each neck edge every 4th row 3 (3, 3, 0, 0) times.
7. Continue working in St st until piece measures the same as Back.
8. Bind off remaining sts.

Sleeve (make 2)

Cast on 18 (20, 20, 22, 22) sts

1. Work in St st, increasing as noted in step 2.
2. How to work inc row: Work 1 st, m 1, work to last st, m 1, work last st.

You will be working inc row on rows noted: 6th (8th, 8th, 6th, 6th) row 3 (5, 5, 3, 3) times. Then inc every 8th (10th, 10th, 8th 8th) rows 4 (1, 1, 4, 4) times.

Sizes
Petite (Small, Medium, Large, X-Large)

Completed Chest Measurements
32 (34, 36, 38, 40)"

Materials
~385 (440, 440, 495, 495) yd/352 (402, 402, 452, 452) m super chunky weight yarn
~Size US 13 needles
~Size J/6.0 mm crochet hook for crocheting neckline
~Finishing needle

Abbreviation Key

beg	beginning
dec	decrease
inc	increase
K	knit
K2tog	Knit 2 stitches together
m 1	Make 1 (inc)
P	Purl
st(s)	stitch(es)
St st	Stockinette stitch

Sample was knitted in Collinette Point 5 (3.5 oz/100 g, 55 yd/50 m per hank; 100% wool) in Pierro.

Gauge
9 sts and 12 rows to 4" over St st (K 1 row, P 1 row) on size 13 needles, or size needed to obtain gauge

Sleeve Knitting Shorthand for size Small. Row:

Row	
1	
2	
3	
4	
5	
6	inc each end
7	
8	
9	
10	
11	
12	inc each end
13	
14	
15	
16	
17	
18	inc each end
19	
20	
21	
22	
23	
24	
25	
26	inc each end
27	
28	
29	
30	
31	
32	
33	
34	inc each end
35	
36	
37	
38	
39	
40	
41	
42	inc each end
43	
44	
45	
46	
47	
48	
49	
50	inc each end

3. Continue working in St st until piece measures 17" from beg.

4. Begin cap shaping as follows: Bind off 2 (3, 3, 3, 3) sts at beg of next 2 rows.

5. Dec 1 st at beg and end of every other row 1 (2, 2, 2, 2) times. Then dec 1 st at beg and end of every row 7 (5, 6, 7, 7) times.

Cap Knitting Shorthand for size Small. Row:

Row	
1	dec at beg & end
2	Knit
3	dec at beg & end
4	dec at beg & end
5	dec at beg & end
6	dec at beg & end
7	dec at beg & end
8	dec at beg & end

6. Bind off 1 st at beg of next 4 rows.

7. Bind off remaining sts.

Finishing

Note before finishing: Refer to Lesson 22, "Getting It All Together" (page 147), for instructions on various finishing techniques.

1. Sew shoulder seams together using horizontal-to-horizontal mattress st.

2. Sew sleeve top to armhole, easing to fit using vertical-to-horizontal mattress st.

3. Sew side and sleeve seams using vertical-to-vertical mattress st.

4. Single crochet around neckline for a clean look (see page 152 for crochet help).

5. Weave in all yarn ends.

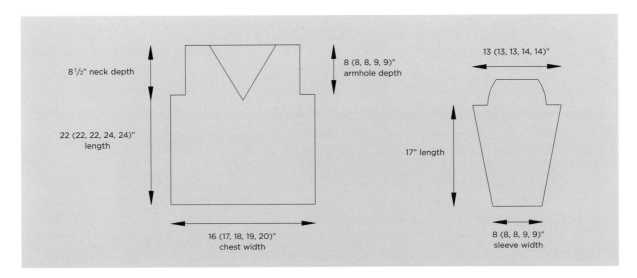

8½" neck depth

8 (8, 8, 9, 9)" armhole depth

22 (22, 22, 24, 24)" length

16 (17, 18, 19, 20)" chest width

13 (13, 13, 14, 14)"

17" length

8 (8, 8, 9, 9)" sleeve width

HORSE OF A DIFFERENT COLOR

Remember watching *The Wizard of Oz*? Dorothy, Toto, and Aunt Em, all in black-and-white; then Dorothy lands in Oz and—POOF! The movie springs to life with all that color! What would the Yellow Brick Road, Emerald City, and Dorothy's ruby slippers have been like if we couldn't view them in full color? We don't know a woman alive who hasn't coveted those red shoes! Well, knitting with color is just like that: By adding a few stripes or even striping every row a different color, you can take a project from so-so to sumptuous and exciting. When knitting with color you may find yourself knitting even faster just to see what the next rows will bring. Remember: You are the artist and knitting is your canvas!

CHANGING COLORS

Changing colors for striping is done the same way as if you were adding on a new ball of yarn. Here's how it's done: To join the new color yarn, leave at least a 6″ tail from the existing yarn and loosely tie the new yarn to it, leaving another 6″ tail. Later, when your project is finished, you can untie the knot and weave both ends into the piece.

Stripe-it-Rich Pillow

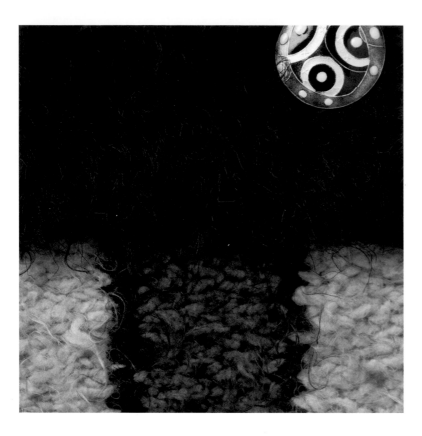

Beginner

Completed Measurements

Approximately 15" x 15"

Materials

~ 255 yd/233 m heavy worsted weight
  yarn in black (A)

~ 85 yd/78 m heavy worsted weight
  yarn in green (B)

~ 85 yd/78 m heavy worsted weight
  yarn in gray (C)

~ Size US 10 needles

~ 3 buttons

~ 15" x 15" pillow form

~ Finishing needle

Abbreviation Key

K	Knit
P	Purl
st(s)	stitch(es)
St st	Stockinette stitch

*Sample was knitted in GGH Esprit (1.75 oz/
50 g, 85 yd/78 m per ball; 100% polyamide,
nylon polyamide) in Black, Celadon, and
Charcoal.*

Gauge

14 sts and 12 rows to 4" over St st
(K 1 row, P 1 row) on size 10 needles, or size needed to obtain gauge

CHICK FEED

This is one tricky little pillow! At first glance it looks as if
you would be knitting across the row and would need to
change colors every few stitches. Instead, we knitted the
front panel sideways and the colors in rows so you only
have to work with one color at a time. Knitting with different colors makes your knitting come to life and is a great
way to express your creativity. We always enjoy seeing the
colors play off of each other, as well as the excitement of
working with different materials. Don't be surprised if you
find yourself knitting much faster because you can't wait
to get to the next color!

Back

Using color A, cast on 52 sts

1. Work in St st (K 1 row, P 1 row) for 26″.
2. Bind off loosely.

Front

Using color A, cast on 50 sts

1. Work in St st for 5 rows.
2. Continuing to work in St st, change to color B, work for 8 rows.
3. Change to color A, work for 2 rows.
4. Change to color C, work for 8 rows.
5. Change to color A, work for 2 rows.
6. Change to color B, work for 12 rows.
7. Change to color A, work for 2 rows.
8. Change to color C, work for 8 rows.
9. Change to color A, work for 2 rows.
10. Change to color B, work for 8 rows.
11. Change to color A, work for 5 rows.
12. Bind off loosely.

Finishing

Note before finishing: Refer to Lesson 22, "Getting It All Together" (page 147), for instructions on various finishing techniques.

1. Lay Back right side down, with cast-on edge at bottom.
2. Fold Back approximately 1 1/2″ from bottom, as shown in diagram.
3. With right side up, lay Front on top of Back, with cast-on edge on left side and bind-off edge on right, as shown in diagram.
4. Stitch Front to Back at side seams and bottom at stitch line as shown in diagram using vertical-to-horizontal mattress st.
5. Insert pillow form and fold top of Back over Front approximately 7 1/2″. Stitch side pieces down.
6. Attach buttons.
7. Weave in all yarn ends.

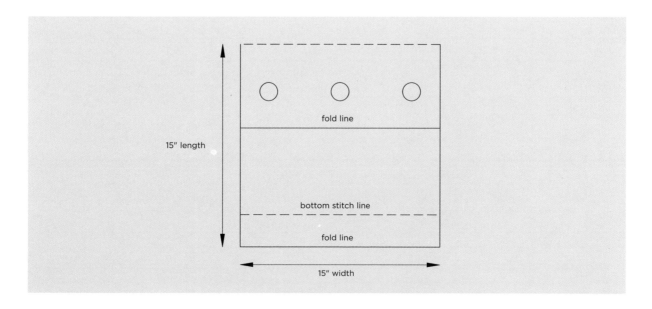

15″ length

fold line

bottom stitch line

fold line

15″ width

Bohemian Felted Hobo Bag

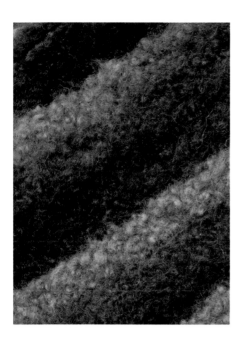

CHICK FEED

This makes a great knitting bag to tote all your projects. You'll get to practice your decreasing skills and then try out the felting process. If you're feeling ambitious, why not knit up the Bohemian Felted Needle Case and the Scoop Bag as well and then felt all three projects together!

Advanced Beginner

Completed Measurements

Approximately 23" wide x 18" long at center to bottom point before felting
Approximately 16" wide x 13" long at center to bottom point after felting

Materials

~ 276 yd/252 m heavy worsted weight yarn in dark brown (A)
~ 138 yd/126 m heavy worsted weight yarn in light green (B)
~ 138 yd/126 m heavy worsted weight yarn in dark green (C)
~ Size US 13 24" circular needles

Note

Bag is knit back and forth, as with straight needles, but circular needles allow you to hold more stitches so you are able to knit more comfortably.

Abbreviation Key

beg	beginning
K	Knit
K2tog	Knit 2 stitches together
m 1	Make 1 (inc)
P	Purl
sl st	slip stitch
st(s)	stitch(es)
tbl	through back loop

Sample was knitted in Manos del Uruguay wool (3.5 oz/100 g, 138 yd/126 m per hank; 100% wool) in Thrush, Citric, and Olive.

Gauge

11 sts and 16 rows to 4" over st pattern on size 13 needles, or size needed to obtain gauge

Stitch Guide

• Slip 1 Stitch (sl 1): Slip stitch from left-hand needle onto right-hand needle without knitting the stitch.
• Knit 2 Together Through Back Loop (K2tog tbl): Insert right-hand needle into back of 2 stitches at the same time, then Knit these stitches together.
• Make 1 increase (m 1): Pick up the horizontal bar between 2 stitches by inserting left-hand needle from back to front and then Knit this stitch.

Stitch Pattern

~ Row 1 K1, K2tog, K34, m 1, sl 1, m 1, K34, K2tog tbl, sl 1, K2tog, K34, m 1, sl 1, m 1, K34, K2tog tbl, sl 1, K1.
~ Row 2 Purl.
~ Row 3 K1, K2tog, K34, m 1, sl 1, m 1, K34, K2tog tbl, sl 1, K2tog, K34, m 1, sl 1, m 1, K34, K2 tbl, sl 1, K1.
~ Row 4 K1, P1, K36, P1, K36, P1, K36, P1, K37.

Bag

Using color A, cast on 150 sts

1. Work Rows 1–4 of st pattern 2 times.
2. Change to color B, work Rows 1–4 of st pattern once.
3. Change to color C, work Rows 1–4 of st pattern once.
4. Change to color A, work Rows 1–4 of st pattern once.
5. Change to color B, work Rows 1–4 of st pattern 2 times.
6. Change to color C, work Rows 1–4 of st pattern once.
7. Change to color A, work Rows 1–4 of st pattern once.
8. Change to color B, work Rows 1–4 of st pattern once.
9. Change to color C, work Rows 1–4 of st pattern 2 times.
10. Change to color A, work Rows 1–4 of st pattern once.
11. Change to color B, work Rows 1–4 of st pattern once.
12. Change to color C, work Rows 1–4 of st pattern once.
13. Change to color A, work Rows 1–4 of st pattern once.
14. Bind off in st pattern.

Strap

Using color A, cast on 20 sts

1. Knit every row until piece measures approximately 40" from beg.
2. Bind off.

Finishing

Note before finishing: Refer to Lesson 22, "Getting It All Together" (page 147), for instructions on various finishing techniques.

1. Fold bag in half lengthwise as shown in diagram.
2. Sew together bottom and side edges using vertical-to-vertical and horizontal-to-horizontal mattress st.
3. Felt bag and strap.
4. When shaped and dried thoroughly, stitch strap to inside of bag on either side using whipstitch.
5. You may line your bag with material if desired. Choosing a coordinating material will enhance the colors of your bag.

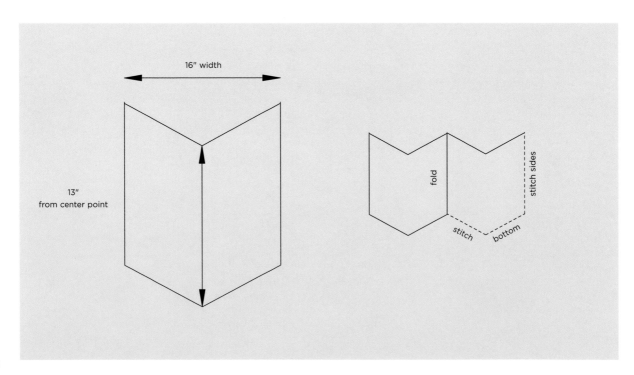

16" width

13"
from center point

fold

stitch sides

stitch   bottom

Bohemian Felted Needle Case

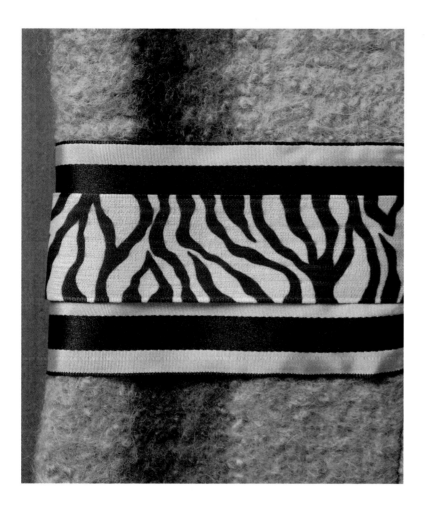

CHICK FEED

If you've already made a few of the projects in this book, your needle assortment has probably grown quite a bit by now. This felted needle case is the perfect handy accessory to store, protect, and organize your needles. It's a quick project that you will felt and then line with a coordinating fabric.

Completed Measurements
Approximately 16" x 20" before felting
Approximately 13" x 16" after felting

Materials
~ 138 yd/126 m heavy worsted weight yarn in yellow (A)
~ 50 yd/46 m heavy worsted weight yarn in green (B)
~ 50 yd/46 m heavy worsted weight yarn in brown (C)
~ Size US 13 needles
~ Approximately ½ yard fabric
~ Approximately 48 inches wide fabric ribbon

Abbreviation Key

K	Knit
P	Purl
St st	Stockinette stitch
st(s)	stitch(es)

Sample was knitted in Manos del Uruguay wool (3.5 oz/100 g, 138 yd/126 m per hank; 100% wool) in Citric, Olive, and Brown.

Gauge
12 sts and 16 rows to 4" over St st (K 1 row, P 1 row) on size 13 needle, or size needed to obtain gauge

Case

Using color A, cast on 60 sts

1. Work in St st for 26 rows.
2. Continuing in St st, change to color B, work for 4 rows.
3. Change to color C, work for 4 rows.
4. Change to color A, work for 46 more rows.
5. Bind off loosely.
6. Felt case.

Finishing

1. If case ends up with wavy sides after felting, let it air-dry completely. Then trim sides with pair of scissors so sides are square.
2. Cut 2 pieces of fabric, one 14″ x 17″ and another 14″ x 11″.
3. Turn under a 1/2″ seam allowance around all edges of both pieces, and press with iron.
4. Place pieces right side up and place smaller piece on top of larger piece. Pin together.
5. Sew into place around sides and bottom by hand or by machine. You will now have one large pocket. To create the smaller pockets, begin at the bottom edge of larger pocket and sew separate vertical seams to top edge of pocket. We spaced our pockets at varying widths to accommodate different needle sizes.
6. Sew fabric onto felted case. We used a sewing machine to sew all the fabric onto the case, but you can just as easily use hand stitching.
7. Cut piece of ribbon approximately 48″ long, attach to outside of case on one edge where case is top stitched. Fold case and tie ribbon in a bow.

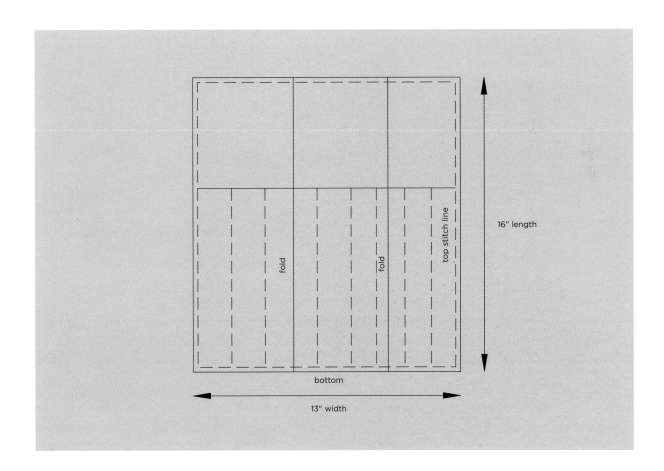

Itchin'-to-Knit Sweater

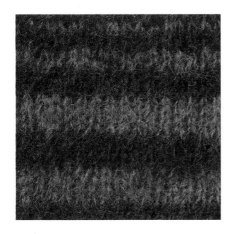

Back

Using color A, cast on 64 (68, 72, 78, 82) sts

1. Knit 3 rows.
2. Change to St st beg with a Knit row. Work for 18 more rows.
3. Continuing to work in St st, change to color B, work for 6 rows.
4. Change to color A, work for 6 rows.
5. Change to color B, work for 4 rows.
6. Change to color A, work for 4 rows.
7. Change to color B, work for 4 rows.
8. Change to color A, work for 3 rows.
9. Change to color B, work for 3 rows.
10. Change to color A, work for 2 rows.
11. Change to color B, work for 2 rows.
12. Change to color A, work 1 row.
13. Change to color B, continue to work until piece measures 13" or desired length from beg. (See "Cheep Tricks" for lengthening and shortening guidance.)
14. Begin armhole shaping as follows: Bind off 3 (4, 4, 5, 5) sts at beg of next 2 rows. Dec 1 st (K2tog), at beg and end of every other row 2 (3, 4, 4, 5) times. Work in St st until piece measures 21 (21, 21, 22, 22)" from beg.
15. Bind off loosely.

Sizes

Petite (Small, Medium, Large, X-Large)

Completed Chest Measurements
32 (34, 36, 38, 40)"

Materials
- ~760 (760, 855, 950, 1,045) yd/ 695 (695, 782, 869, 956) m heavy worsted weight mohair in mauve (A)
- ~190 yd/174 m heavy worsted weight mohair in purple (B)
- ~Size US 9 needles
- ~Size J/6.0 mm crochet hook for crocheted neckline
- ~Finishing needle

Abbreviation Key

beg	beginning
dec	decrease
inc	increase
K	Knit
K2tog	Knit 2 stitches together
P	Purl
st(s)	stitch(es)
St st	Stockinette stitch

Sample was knitted in Jo Sharp, Kid Mohair (.88 oz/25 g, 95 yd/87 m per ball; 80% kid mohair, 5% wool polyamide) in #604 Mauve and #603 Eggplant.

Gauge

16 sts and 22 rows to 4" over St st (K 1 row, P 1 row) on size 9 needles, or size needed to obtain gauge

CHICK FEED

It's amazing what a little gauge can do! Essentially, this is the same sweater as the Five Below Sweater (see page 70), but it is knit with thinner yarn and smaller needles, and we've added a few stripes for visual interest. Often new knitters don't understand the importance of gauge; but if you compare the two sweaters, you'll see clearly that changing the thickness of the yarn and the needle size can really alter a pattern.

CHEEP TRICKS

At step 13 you can add or subtract a few inches if you would like to lengthen or shorten the sweater. Keep in mind that if you choose to lengthen, you will be using more yarn. Adjusting length is quite easy. Decide how many inches you would like your garment to be by measuring a favorite old sweater in your closet. The measurement should be from under the arm to the bottom edge of the sweater. This will tell you how many inches you need to adjust the pattern. Then when the pattern instructs you to work so many inches until the armhole, use your own measurements, whether they are more or less than the pattern states.

Front

Using color A, cast on 64 (68, 72, 78, 82) sts

1. Knit 3 rows.
2. Change to St st beg with a Knit row. Work for 18 more rows.
3. Change to color B, work for 6 rows.
4. Change to color A, work for 6 rows.
5. Change to color B, work for 4 rows.
6. Change to color A, work for 4 rows.
7. Change to color B, work for 4 rows.
8. Change to color A, work for 3 rows.
9. Change to color B, work for 3 rows.
10. Change to color A, work for 2 rows.
11. Change to color B, work for 2 rows.
12. Change to color A, work 1 row.
13. Change to color B, continue work until piece measures 13" or desired length from beg.
14. Begin armhole shaping as follows: Bind off 3 (4, 4, 5, 5) sts at beg of next 2 rows.
15. Dec 1 st (K2tog) at beg and end of every other row 2 (3, 4, 4, 5) times.
16. Begin neck shaping as follows: Work 27 (27, 28, 30, 31) sts, attach a new ball of yarn. With new yarn, work remaining sts. You now will be working both sides of the shoulders at the same time, each side using its own ball of yarn.
17. Dec 1 st at each neck edge every 2nd (2nd, 2nd, 3rd, 3rd) row 7 (5, 5, 6, 6) times. Then dec 1 st at each neck edge every 4th row 6 (8, 8, 7, 7) times.
18. Continue working in St st until piece measures same as Back.

Sleeves (make 2)

Using color B, cast on 32 (32, 32, 36, 36) sts

1. Knit 3 rows.
2. Change to St st, increasing as noted in step 3.
3. How to work inc row: Work 1 st, m 1, work to last st, m 1, work last st.

You will be working inc row on rows noted: Work this inc every 8th (8th, 6th, 8th, 7th) row 6 (6, 4, 2, 8) times. Then inc every 10th (10th, 8th, 9th, 8th) row 4 (4, 8, 8, 4) times.

4. Continue working in st pattern until piece measures 17" from beg.
5. Begin cap shaping as follows: Bind off 3 (4, 4, 5, 5) sts at beg of next 2 rows.
6. Dec 1 st at beg and end of every other row 2 (3, 4, 7, 15) times. Then dec 1 st at beg and end of every row (every 2nd, 4th, 3rd, 0) row 9 (3, 1, 6, 0) times.
7. Bind off 2 (2, 3, 0, 0) sts at beg of next 4 rows.
8. Bind off remaining sts loosely in st pattern.

Finishing

Note before finishing: Refer to Lesson 22, "Getting It All Together" (page 147), for instructions on various finishing techniques.

1. Sew shoulder seams together using horizontal-to-horizontal mattress st.
2. Sew sleeve top to armholes, easing to fit using vertical-to-horizontal mattress st.
3. Sew side and sleeve seams using vertical-to-vertical mattress st.
4. Single crochet around neckline for a finished look.
5. Weave in all yarn ends.

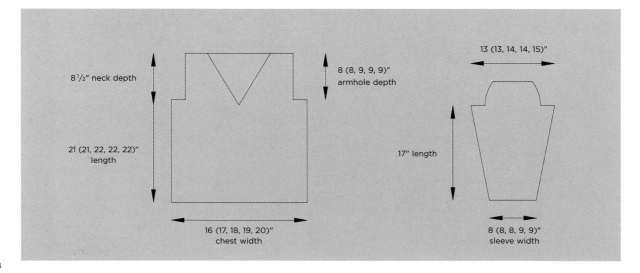

8 1/2" neck depth

8 (8, 9, 9, 9)" armhole depth

13 (13, 14, 14, 15)"

21 (21, 22, 22, 22)" length

17" length

16 (17, 18, 19, 20)" chest width

8 (8, 8, 9, 9)" sleeve width

Lesson 10

STICK OUT YOUR RIBS!

~~~~~~

RIB STITCH (K1, P1 OR 1 x 1 RIB)

The ribbing that results from knitting in rib stitch puts stretch into your work. Its elasticity makes it perfect for necklines and edges of garments. A rib stitch can consist of a Knit 1, Purl 1 or Knit 2, Purl 2 combination, or however many stitches you desire for your ribbing. Just keep in mind that the wider the rib pattern, the less stretch the knitting will have.

Try a sample K1, P1 rib:

~ **Row 1 Knit 1 st , Purl 1 st, repeat across row.**

~ **Row 2 Knit the Knit stitches and Purl the Purl stitches.**

~ **Repeat these 2 rows until you reach the desired length.**

Coed Ribbed Scarf

CHICK FEED

Our Coed Ribbed Scarf is aptly named because it can be worn by women and men alike. We knitted it in a repetitive 2 x 2 rib pattern. This stitch pattern is great for scarves because it looks fabulous on both sides. Knit in a very soft brushed alpaca, this scarf is certain to keep the wearer cozy.

Beginner

Completed Measurements

Approximately 5" x 54"

Materials

- ~ 330 yd/302 m heavy worsted weight yarn in red (A)
- ~ 110 yd/100 m heavy worsted weight yarn in orange (B)
- ~ Size US 8 needles

Sample was knitted in Plymouth Baby Alpaca Brush (1.75 oz/50 g, 110 yd/100 m per ball; 80% baby alpaca, 20% acrylic) in #2120 Tomato and #1004 Pumpkin.

Abbreviation Key

K	Knit
P	Purl
st(s)	stitch(es)

Gauge

18 sts and 22 rows to 4" over St st (K 1 row, P 1 row) on size 8 needles, or size needed to obtain gauge

Stitch Guide:
K2, P2 Rib Pattern

- ~ Row 1 Knit 2, Purl 2. Repeat across row.
- ~ Row 2 Knit the Knit stitches and Purl the Purl stitches.
- ~ Repeat Rows 1 and 2.

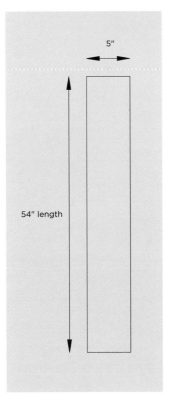

5"

54" length

Scarf

Using color A, cast on 34 sts

1. Work in Knit 2, Purl 2 Rib Pattern for 12 rows.
2. Continuing to work in st pattern, change to color B, work for 4 rows.
3. Change to color A, work for 4 rows.
4. Change to color B, work for 2 rows.
5. Change to color A, work for 4 rows.
6. Change to color B, work for 4 rows.
7. Change to color A, work for 2 rows.
8. Change to color B, work for 2 rows.
9. Change to color A, work for 40".
10. Change to color B, work for 2 rows.
11. Change to color A, work for 2 rows.
12. Change to color B, work for 4 rows.
13. Change to color A, work for 4 rows.
14. Change to color B, work for 2 rows.
15. Change to color A, work for 4 rows.
16. Change to color B, work for 4 rows.
17. Change to color A, work for 12 rows.
18. Bind off in st pattern.
19. Weave in all yarn ends.

Coed Ribbed Wrist Warmers

Wrist warmers have gained so much popularity due to our need to keep our fingers free to tap the keys on our cell phones. These little warmers keep your hands cozy but your fingers free to send a text message. Ours were knit to match the Coed Ribbed Scarf; make the set for a great gift!

Wrist Warmers (make 2)

Using color A, cast on 32 sts

1. Work in K2, P2 Rib Pattern for 9 rows.
2. Continuing to work in st pattern, change to color B, work for 4 rows.
3. Change to color A, work for 4 rows.
4. Change to color B, work for 2 rows.
5. Change to color A, work for 4 rows.
6. Change to color B, work for 4 rows.
7. Change to color A, work for 2 rows.
8. Change to color B, work for 2 rows.
9. Change to color A, work for 15 rows.
10. Bind off in st pattern.
11. Weave in all yarn ends.

Finishing

Note before finishing: Refer to Lesson 22, "Getting It All Together" (page 147), for instructions on various finishing techniques.

1. Sew seam using vertical-to-vertical mattress st for approximately 4".
2. Leave approximately 1" to 1 ½" opening for thumb.
3. Continue to stitch seam to end.
4. Weave in all yarn ends.

Beginner

Size

One size fits most

Completed Measurements

8" x 6"

Materials

~ 110 yd/100 m heavy worsted weight yarn in red (A)

~ 50 yd/46 m heavy worsted weight yarn in orange (B)

~ Size US 6 needles

Sample was knitted in Plymouth Baby Alpaca Brush (1.75 oz/50 g, 110 yd/100 m per ball; 80% baby alpaca, 20% acrylic) in #2120 Tomato and #1004 Pumpkin.

Abbreviation Key

K	Knit
P	Purl
st(s)	stitch(es)
St st	Stockinette stitch

Gauge

21 sts and 26 rows to 4" over St st (K 1 row, P 1 row) on size 6 needle, or size needed to obtain gauge

Stitch Guide:
K2, P2 Rib Pattern

~ Row 1 Knit 2, Purl 2. Repeat across row.

~ Row 2 Knit the Knit stitches and Purl the Purl stitches.

~ Repeat Rows 1 and 2.

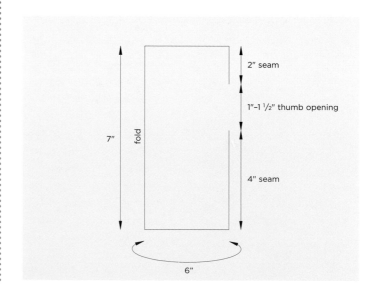

Lesson 11

PICK IT UP

PICKING UP STITCHES

Learning how to pick up stitches is an essential step in learning to knit. This technique is used to add necklines and front button bands to sweaters after a garment is constructed by picking up stitches along the finished edge to create a row of new stitches. When you are picking up stitches for a button band or along the front of a sweater, you are picking up stitches in the rows vertically. When you are picking up stitches along a neckline, you will be working horizontally, picking up a stitch in an existing stitch.

Neckline (Horizontal)

1. Place your work with the right side facing up. Starting at the right edge of your knitted piece, hold the needle in your right hand and insert the needle into the middle of the V of the first stitch.
2. Using newly attached yarn, wrap the yarn around the needle as if to Knit (counterclockwise).
3. Bring the loop of the working yarn through to the right side of the project.
4. Repeat steps 1–3, working horizontally for the entire edge to be picked up.

Front Edge (Vertical)

1. Place your work with the right side facing up. Starting at the right edge of your knitted piece, hold the needle in your right hand and insert the needle into the first stitch.
2. Using newly attached yarn, wrap the yarn around the needle as if to Knit (counterclockwise).
3. Bring the loop of the working yarn through to the right side of the project.
4. Repeat steps 1–3, working vertically along the row of the front edge.

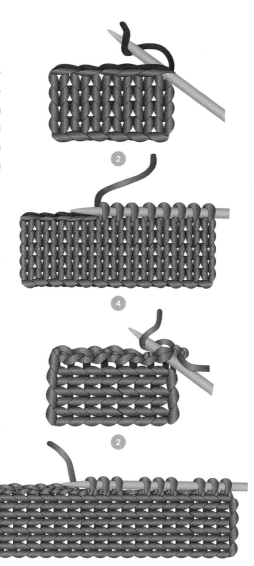

Chill Out Wrap

CHICK FEED

This isn't Granny's old shawl! We've modernized the pattern, now known as a *wrap*, by using a sumptuous brushed alpaca and adding a little ruffled edge. Wraps are fun to knit because they are relatively simple patterns. You'll be able to relax, watch TV, chat with friends, and enjoy yourself while knitting this project. It will look great with just about anything you pair it with, from jeans to evening attire.

Advanced Beginner

Completed Measurements
Approximately 64" wide x 26" long at point

Materials
~ 550 yd/502 m heavy worsted weight yarn in brown
~ Size US 10 needles
~ Size US 10 24" circular needles
~ Finishing needle

Abbreviation Key

inc	increase
K	Knit
kfb	Knit in front, then in back of same stitch
m 1	Make 1 (inc)
P	Purl
st(s)	stitch(es)
St st	Stockinette stitch

Sample was knitted in Plymouth Baby Alpaca Brush (1.75 oz/50 g, 110 yd/100 m per ball; 80% baby alpaca, 20% acrylic) in Brown.

Gauge
14 sts and 19 rows to 4" over St st (K 1 row, P 1 row) on size 10 needles, or size needed to obtain gauge

Wrap

Stitch Guide: Make 1 Increase (m 1)

The increase in this pattern is done by picking up the horizontal bar between two stitches. You will be using this method for both the Knit row and the Purl row.

Using size 10 straight needles, cast on 3 sts
- Row 1 K1, m 1, Knit remaining sts across row—this is the right side.
- Row 2 P1, m 1, Purl remaining sts across row—this is the wrong side.
- Repeat Rows 1 and 2 until there are 80 sts on needle. End with a wrong side row.

Next Section

- Row 1 K1, m 1, Knit across row to last st, m 1, Knit last st.
- Row 2 P1, m 1, Purl across row to last st, m 1, Purl last st.
- Repeat Rows 1 and 2 until there are 200 sts on needle.
- Bind off very loosely. (You will want to bind off loosely to allow the top edge of the shawl to stretch to the right proportion.)

Ruffled Edge

Stitch Guide: kfb increase

This increase is done by knitting in the front and back of the same stitch. Insert the needle into the next stitch, Knit that stitch but do not take the stitch off the needle. Now insert the needle into the back of that same stitch and Knit this stitch again. This will create another stitch.

Picking Up Stitches and Working Ruffled Edge

1. With right side facing and using size 10 circular needles and starting at the bottom point of the shawl, pick up and Knit the stitches horizontally along side edge of shawl.
2. Next row: Purl.
3. Next row: *Knit 1, inc 1 stitch (kfb) in next stitch*. Repeat from * to * across row.
4. Work in St st for 10 rows.
5. Bind off.
6. Repeat steps 1–5 for the opposite side of the shawl.

Finishing

Note before finishing: Refer to Lesson 22, "Getting It All Together" (page 147), for instructions on various finishing techniques.

1. Sew ruffle together at bottom point using vertical-to-vertical mattress st.
2. Weave in all yarn ends.

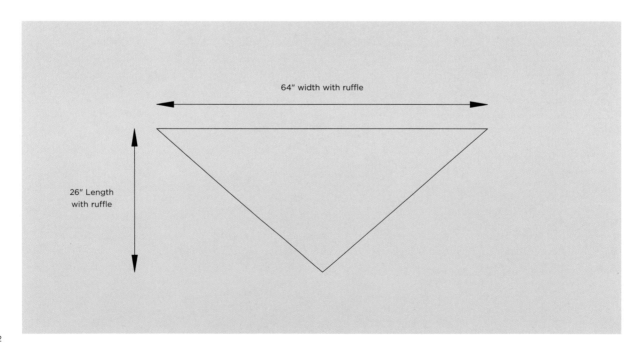

64" width with ruffle

26" Length
with ruffle

Bone-i-fied Dog Sweater

CHICK FEED

Pamper your pooch with an adorable sweater. You can choose whichever colors fit your dog's personality: Try pink, green, or white if she's preppy, or combine the colors of his favorite sports team, or even try all black if your pup has a darker, devious side. . . . You get the idea. This is a project to really have fun with. We do recommend using a washable yarn so your little dog can have just as much fun wearing it.

Advanced Beginner

Size
Small

Completed Chest Measurement
17"

Completed Length Measurement
16"

Note
There's a lot of variation in the shapes and sizes of small dogs, so you may need to add or subtract inches from the length to custom fit your pooch.

Materials
~ 74 yd/68 m heavy worsted weight yarn in pink (A)
~ 74 yd/68 m heavy worsted weight yarn in purple (B)
~ 74 yd/68 m heavy worsted weight yarn in green (C)
~ Size US 8 needles
~ Size US 8 24" circular needles
~ Finishing needle

Abbreviation Key

beg	beginning
dec	decrease
K	Knit
K2tog	Knit 2 stitches together
m 1	Make 1 (inc)
P	Purl
st(s)	stitch(es)
St st	Stockinette stitch

Sample was knitted in The Sassy Skein, Key West Karibbean Kotton Kollection (74 yd/68 m per ball; 100% mercerized cotton) in #206 Flamingo-pink, #205 Wild Iris-purple, and #207 Kiwi-green.

Gauge
18 sts and 24 rows to 4" over St st (K 1 row, P 1 row) on size 8 needles, or size needed to obtain gauge

Stitch Guide:
Make 1 Increase (m 1)
The increase in this pattern is done by picking up the horizontal bar between two stitches by inserting the left-hand needle from back to front and then Knit or Purl (depending on the row) this stitch. You will be using this method for both the Knit row and the Purl row.
~Knit 1, Make 1 stitch, Knit across to last stitch, Make 1 stitch, Knit last stitch—this is the right side.
~Purl 1, Make 1 stitch, Purl across to last stitch, Make 1 stitch, Purl last stitch—this is the wrong side.

Collar

Using size 8 straight needles and color C, cast on 52 sts

1. Work in K1, P1 Rib Pattern for 8 rows. (K1, P1. Repeat across row.)
2. Change to St st.
3. *K5, m 1*. Repeat from * to * across row, Knit remaining sts (total 62 sts).
4. Continue working in St st for 2 more rows.

Body

Color Sequence (for Body): Alternate color A and color B every 4 rows

1. Continuing to work in St st and using color A (color sequence begins), m 1 at beg and end of next row, and every following 4th row 7 times (total 78 sts).
2. Work in St st even for 36 more rows (remembering to alternate colors every 4 rows).
3. Begin Back shaping as follows: Bind off 15 sts at beg of next 2 rows.
4. Work even in St st for 2 more rows.
5. Dec 1 st (K2tog) at beg and end of next row and every other row 7 more times.
6. Work even until piece measures 16" from beg, or desired length for your pooch.
7. Bind off remaining sts.

Bottom Hem

1. Sew center front seam from top of collar to beg of back shaping using vertical-to-vertical mattress st (see page 151).
2. Using size 8 circular needles and color C and with right side facing up, start at center seam and pick up approximately 50 sts along first side of back shaping, 32 sts along bottom of back shaping, and 50 sts along second side of back shaping. (Remember, this is just an approximate number of stitches; you will need to pick up more stitches if you adjust the length.)
3. Work in K1, P1 Rib Pattern for 7 rows.
4. Bind off loosely in st pattern.

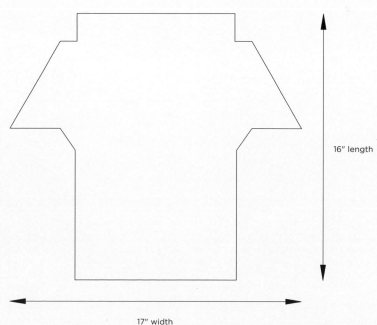

16" length

17" width

Guy's Tailgate Sweater

Back

Using size 10 straight needles and color A, cast on 84 (92, 100) sts

1. Work in K2, P2 Rib Pattern for 16 rows.
2. Change to St st, work for 26 rows.
3. Continuing to work in St st, change to color B, work for 20 rows.
4. Change to color A, work for 20 rows.
5. Change to color B, work for 20 rows.
6. Change to color A, work for 3 rows.
7. Begin armhole shaping as follows (working in same color): Bind off 5 (6, 7) sts at beg of next 2 rows.
8. Dec 1 st (K2tog) at beg and end of every other row 4 times.
9. Continue working in St st with color A for 7 more rows.
10. Change to color B, work for 20 rows.
11. Change to color A, work for 17 (19, 19) rows.
12. Bind off remaining sts.

Front

Using Color A and size 10 straight needles, cast on 84 (92, 100) sts

1. Work in K2, P2 Rib Pattern for 16 rows.
2. Change to St st, work for 26 rows.

Advanced Beginner

Sizes

Medium (Large, X-Large)

Completed Chest Measurements

42 (46, 50)"

Materials

~ 720 (840, 960) yd/658 (768, 878) m heavy worsted weight yarn in olive green (A)
~ 540 (660, 780) yd/494 (604, 713) m heavy worsted weight yarn in kiwi green (B)
~ Size US 10 needles
~ Size US 10 16" circular needles
~ Finishing needle

Abbreviation Key

beg	beginning
dec	decrease
inc	increase
K	Knit
K2tog	Knit 2 stitches together
m 1	Make 1 (inc)
P	Purl
st(s)	stitch(es)
St st	Stockinette stitch

Sample was knitted in Cleckheaton, Merino Supreme (1.75 oz/50 g, 62 yd/57 m per ball; 100% Australian pure new wool) in colors #2205 and #2222.

Gauge

16 sts and 22 rows over 4" St st (K 1 row, P 1 row) on size 10 needles, or size needed to obtain gauge

Stitch Guide:
K2, P2 Rib Pattern

~ Row 1 Knit 2, Purl 2. Repeat across row.
~ Row 2 Knit the Knit stitches and Purl the Purl stitches.
~ Repeat Rows 1 and 2.

CHICK FEED

By now the man in your life has probably looked over your shoulder a few times and asked when you will make something for him. Believe it or not, sweater patterns for men are few and far between, so we took inspiration from a few great sweaters we found in some of our favorite men's stores. This sweater has a casual, relaxed fit and will look great on just about everyone . . . so don't be afraid to "borrow" it after he's worn it a few times! If you are a little apprehensive about the color changes in this pattern, it will look just as great knitted in a solid color.

3. Continuing to work in St st, change to color B, work for 20 rows.

4. Change to color A, work for 20 rows.

5. Change to color B, work for 20 rows.

6. Change to color A, work for 3 rows.

7. Begin armhole shaping as follows (working in same color): Bind off 5 (6, 7) sts at beg of next 2 rows.

8. Dec 1 st at beg and end of every other row 4 times.

9. Continue working in St st with color A for 7 more rows.

10. Change to color B, work for 20 rows.

11. Change to Color A, work 27 (28, 30) sts, attach a new ball of yarn (same color). With new yarn bind off center 16 (18, 18) sts, work remaining 27 (28, 30) sts. You now will be working both sides of the shoulders at the same time, each side using its own ball of yarn.

12. Dec 1 st at each neck edge every other row 8 times.

13. Continue working in St st for 1 (2, 2) more rows.

14. Bind off remaining sts.

Color Sequence (for sleeves)

1. Working in St st, work color A for 36 rows.

2. Work color B for 20 rows.

3. Work color A for 20 rows.

4. Work color B for 20 rows.

5. Work color A for 20 rows.

6. Work color B for 20 rows.

7. Work color A until you bind off.

Sleeves (make 2)

Using size 10 straight needles and Color Sequence, cast on 42 (46, 48) sts.

1. Work in K2, P2 Rib Pattern for 16 rows.

2. Change to St st, increasing as noted in step 3.

3. How to work inc row: Work 1 st, m 1, work to last st, m 1, work last st.

You will be working inc row on rows noted: every 8th (8th, 6th) row 8 (8, 1) times. Then inc every 10th (10th, 8th) row 3 (3, 11) times.

4. Continue working in Color Sequence until piece measures 18" from beg.

5. Begin cap shaping as follows: Bind off 4 (5, 6) sts at beg of next 2 rows.

6. Dec 1 st at beg and end of every other row 3 (4, 5) times. Then dec 1 st at beg and end of every 2nd (2nd, every) row 12 (12, 7) times.

7. Dec 1 st at beg and end of every 0 (0, 2nd) row 0 (0, 5) times.

8. Bind off 3 sts at beg of next 4 rows.

9. Bind off remaining sts.

Finishing

Note before finishing: Refer to Lesson 22, "Getting It All Together" (page 147), for instructions on various finishing techniques.

1. Sew shoulder seams together using horizontal-to-horizontal mattress st.

2. Sew sleeve top to armhole, easing to fit using vertical-to-horizontal mattress st.

3. Sew side and sleeve seams using vertical-to-vertical mattress st.

4. Weave in all yarn ends.

Neck Finishing

1. Using size 10 circular needles and color A and with right side facing up, start at right shoulder and pick up approximately 86 (90, 92) sts around neckline.

2. Work in K2, P2 Rib Pattern for 6 rows.

3. Bind off loosely in st pattern.

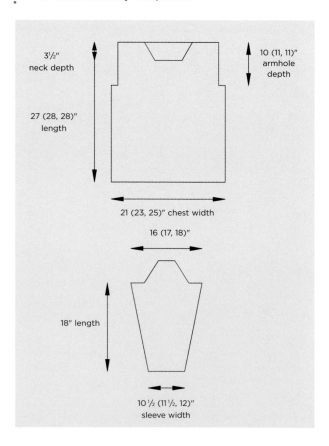

3½"
neck depth

10 (11, 11)"
armhole depth

27 (28, 28)"
length

21 (23, 25)" chest width

16 (17, 18)"

18" length

10 ½ (11 ½, 12)"
sleeve width

Lesson 12

SOW SOME SEEDS

~~~~~~

SEED STITCH

The seed stitch looks exactly like it sounds, a stitch with an all-over texture of little bumps that resemble seeds. It is made by alternating knit and purl stitches, like a checkerboard. It works up great in a scarf because the stitch looks the same from either side, and it will lie flat and not curl around the edges, as with Stockinette stitch. It also makes a nice edge for a garment. Here's how it's done:

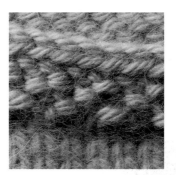

- Row 1 Knit 1 stitch, Purl 1 stitch. Repeat across row.
- Row 2 Purl the Knit stitches and Knit the Purl stitches.
- Repeat Row 2 until desired length.

Town & Country Tee

Back

Using size 7 straight needles, cast on 75 (80, 85, 90, 95, 100) sts

1. Work in Seed Stitch Pattern for 5 rows.
2. Change to St st, work for 87 rows.
3. Begin armhole shaping as follows: Bind off 3 (3, 4, 5, 6, 6) sts at beg of next 2 rows.
4. Dec 1 st (K2tog) at beg and end of every other row 2 (3, 4, 5, 5, 6) times.
5. Continue working in St st until there is a total of 140 (148, 148, 150, 150, 154) rows.
6. Bind off.

Front

Using size 7 straight needles, cast on 75 (80, 85, 90, 95, 100) sts

1. Work in Seed Stitch Pattern for 5 rows.
2. Change to St st, work for 87 rows.
3. Begin armhole shaping as follows: Bind off 3 (3, 4, 5, 6, 6) sts at beg of next 2 rows.
4. Dec 1 st at beg and end of every other row 2 (3, 4, 5, 5, 6) times.
5. Continue working in St st until there is a total of 110 (118, 118, 120, 120, 124) rows.

Sizes

Petite (X-Small, Small, Medium, Large, X-Large)

Completed Chest Measurements

30 (32, 34, 36, 38, 40)"

Materials

~ 625 (625, 750, 750, 875, 875) yd/ 571 (571, 686, 686, 800, 800) m worsted weight yarn in light green
~ Size US 7 needles
~ Size US 7 16" circular needles
~ Finishing needle

Abbreviation Key

beg	beginning
dec	decrease
K	Knit
K2tog	Knit 2 stitches together
P	Purl
st(s)	stitch(es)
St st	Stockinette stitch

Sample was knitted in Classic Elite Lush (1.75 oz/50 g, 124 yd/113 m per ball; 50% angora, 50% wool) in #4474.

Gauge

20 sts and 28 rows to 4" over St st (K 1 row, P 1 row) on size 7 needles, or size needed to obtain gauge

Note

This is a row-counting pattern, so an accurate gauge count is necessary. A row counter will help you keep track of rows.

Stitch Guide:
Seed Stitch Pattern

~ Row 1 Knit 1, Purl 1. Repeat across row.
~ Row 2 Purl the Knit stitches and Knit the Purl stitches.
~ Repeat Row 2.

CHICK FEED

If you're more the type to be on the town, try knitting this tee in silk or cotton and wearing it under a jacket as a layering piece. If you're in the country, change the feel of the tee by knitting it in a wool or angora blend for a casual weekend look. Our Town & Country Tee is stylish yet simple to knit. We've added seed stitch detail on the hems to prevent rolling and to add texture.

6. Begin neck shaping as follows: Work 26 (27, 28, 28, 30, 31) sts, attach a new ball of yarn. With new yarn, bind off center 13 (14, 13, 14, 13, 14) sts, work remaining 26 (27, 28, 28, 30, 31) sts. You now will be working both sides of the shoulders at the same time, each side using its own ball of yarn.

7. Work across first shoulder, bind off 2 sts at neck edge of 2nd shoulder, work remaining sts.

8. Repeat Row 7 for 5 more rows.

9. Dec 1 st at each neck edge every other row 8 (7, 8, 7, 8, 7) times.

10. Continue working in St st until piece measures same as Back.

11. Bind off remaining sts.

Sleeves (make 2)

Using size 7 straight needles, cast on 50 (62, 64, 68, 70, 70) sts

1. Work in Seed Stitch Pattern for 5 rows.

2. Change to St st, work for 14 rows.

3. Begin cap shaping as follows: Bind off 3 (3, 4, 5, 6, 6) sts at beg of next 2 rows.

4. Dec 1 st at beg and end of every other row 11 (9, 7, 8, 12, 13) times. Then dec 1 st at beg and end of every 4th row 1 (3, 4, 4, 2, 2) times.

5. Bind off 2 sts at beg of next 4 rows.

6. Bind off remaining sts.

Finishing

Note before finishing: Refer to Lesson 22, "Getting It All Together" (page 147), for instructions on various finishing techniques.

1. Sew shoulder seams together using horizontal-to-horizontal mattress st.

2. Sew sleeve top to armhole, easing to fit using vertical-to-horizontal mattress st.

3. Sew side and sleeve seams using vertical-to-vertical mattress st.

4. Weave in all yarn ends.

Neck Finishing

1. Using size 7 circular needles and with right side facing up, pick up approximately 124 sts around neck, starting at right shoulder, and work around back.

2. Work in Seed Stitch Pattern for 5 rows.

3. Bind off in st pattern.

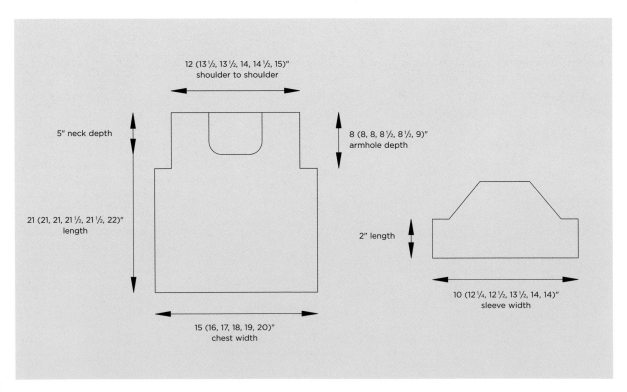

12 (13½, 13½, 14, 14½, 15)" shoulder to shoulder

5" neck depth

8 (8, 8, 8½, 8½, 9)" armhole depth

21 (21, 21, 21½, 21½, 22)" length

2" length

15 (16, 17, 18, 19, 20)" chest width

10 (12¼, 12½, 13½, 14, 14)" sleeve width

Lesson 13

OVER THE YARN WE GO!

YARN OVER (YO)

Yarn over is a simple way to increase that creates a new stitch on your needle and results in a small hole in your work—on purpose! Knitters often use the yarn over increase for lace knitting and to make buttonholes. You can do it in both Knit stitch and Purl stitch, as we'll show you.

Yarn Over Stitch (Knit Row)

Knit 1, wrap yarn UNDER and OVER the right-hand needle (1) (the yarn now should be back in the Knit position), then Knit the next stitch (2). On the following row, just work the yarn over as a regular stitch.

Yarn Over Stitch (Purl Row)

Purl 1, wrap your yarn OVER and UNDER the right-hand needle, ending in the front (3) (the yarn now should be in the Purl position), then Purl the next stitch. On the following row, work the yarn over as a regular stitch.

LATTICE STITCH (P1, YO, P2TOG)

The Lattice stitch is very open and airy and resembles a garden lattice fence. All of the projects we have covered to this point have used stitch patterns that are somewhat traditional, tight, and utilitarian. The Lattice stitch is your first taste of lace knitting. Lace just means that it is open and full of holes. To create those holes, most patterns use a lot of yarn overs and "Knit 2 together" to achieve the look. There are thousands of lace patterns available; we selected this one because it is repetitive and easy to master.

Here's how it's done:
~ Purl 1, *yarn over (yo), Purl 2 together*. Repeat from * to * across to last stitch. Purl last stitch.
~ Repeat Row 1 for all rows.

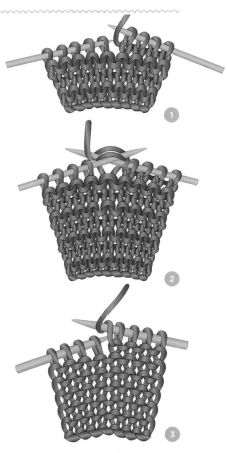

Girls' Night Out Shrug

CHICK FEED

Here's a fun, simple project, but be prepared: All of your friends are going to want one! The Girls' Night Out Shrug is just three rectangles sewn together, but what makes it special is the yarn. We used a ribbon yarn because of the drape and fluidity it offers. There is no shaping to this project; due to the stretch of the stitch and the movement of the ribbon, you'll be able to pull it to tie in the front, secure it with a decorative pin, or just leave it open—it's truly a great layering piece.

Back

Cast on 34 (38, 40) sts

1. Work in Lattice Stitch Pattern until piece measures 15" from beg.
2. Bind off loosely in st pattern.

Front (make 2)

Cast on 16 (18, 20) sts

1. Work in Lattice Stitch Pattern until piece measures 15" from beg.
2. Bind off loosely in st pattern.

Finishing

1. Sew shoulder seams tog beg at outside edge and working in toward neck edge for approximately 3" using whipstitch (see page 152).
2. Sew side seams beg at lower edge for approximately 6", leaving approximately 9" for armhole opening using whipstitch.
3. Weave in all yarn ends.
4. Tie bottom front corners together to close.

Advanced Beginner

Sizes
Small (Medium, Large)

Completed Chest Measurements
32–34 (36–38, 40–42)"

Materials
~ 200 (300, 300) yd/182 (274, 274) m 1/4 ribbon yarn
~ Size US 15 needles
~ Finishing needle

Abbreviation Key

beg	beginning
P	Purl
P2tog	Purl 2 stitches together
st(s)	stitch(es)
tog	together
yo	yarn over

Sample was knitted in Judy & Co, 1/4 Hand-Dyed Rayon Ribbon (100 yds/91 m per hank; 100% rayon) in Amaryllis.

Gauge not necessary

Stitch Guide:
Lattice Stitch Pattern

1. Purl 1, *yo, P2tog*. Repeat from * to * across to last stitch. Purl in last stitch.
2. Repeat Row 1 for all rows.

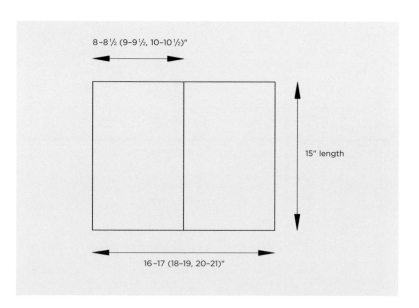

8–8 1/2 (9–9 1/2, 10–10 1/2)"

15" length

16–17 (18–19, 20–21)"

Our Esprit Open Weave Sweater

Back

Cast on 26 (30, 36) sts loosely

1. Work in Lattice Stitch Pattern until piece measures 20″ from beg.
2 Bind off loosely in st pattern.

Front

Cast on 26 (30, 36) sts loosely

1. Work in Lattice Stitch Pattern until piece measures 20″ from beg or same as Back.
2. Bind off loosely in st pattern.

Sleeves (make 2)

Cast on 18 (22, 26) sts loosely

1. Work in Lattice Stitch Pattern until piece measures 19″ from beg.
2. Bind off loosely in st pattern.

Finishing

1. Sew shoulder seams beg at outside edge and working in toward neck edge for approximately 3″ using whipstitch (see page 152).
2. Find center point of top edge of sleeve. Attach this point to seam where shoulders meet with a seaming pin (this will hold the sleeve in place while it is being stitched). Sew sleeves in place along front and back edges using whipstitch.
3. Sew side and sleeve seams using whipstitch.
4. Weave in all yarn ends.

Advanced Beginner

Sizes

Small (Medium, Large)

Completed Chest Measurements

32–34 (36–38, 40–42)"

Materials

~ 340 (340, 425) yd/310 (310, 388) m heavy worsted weight yarn in purple
~ Size US 17 needles
~ Finishing needle

Note on yarn for this project:

We used a heavy worsted weight yarn and made it a super bulky weight yarn by using two strands held together throughout this project. Just keep in mind that IF you decide to do this too, you will need to double the yardage that is called for in the pattern.

Abbreviation Key

beg	beginning
K	Knit
P	Purl
P2tog	Purl 2 stitches together
st(s)	stitch(es)
St st	Stockinette stitch
yo	yarn over

Sample was knitted in GGH Esprit (1.75 oz/50 g, 85 yd/78 m per ball; 100% polyamide nylon) in Eggplant.

Gauge

6.5 sts and 10 rows to 4" over St st (K1 row, P1 row) on size 17 needles, or size needed to obtain gauge

Stitch Guide:
Lattice Stitch Pattern

Purl 1, *yo, P2tog*. Repeat from * to * across to last stitch. Purl last stitch.

CHICK FEED

Can you knit four scarves? If you answered yes, you can knit this project, because it is simply four rectangles sewn together. You don't have to do any shaping because the drape will move with your body. The stitch is lacy and the yarn is fuzzy, so it looks bulky; but it is actually very lightweight, not to mention comfy—it'll fit like your favorite old sweatshirt!

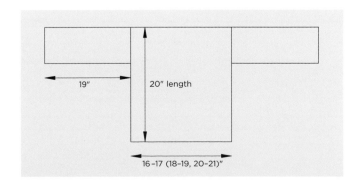

KNITTING IN THE ROUND

~~~~~~

Totally Tubular!

So far you've learned how to knit panels by working back and forth across each row. Now, instead of working back and forth, you will work a tube by knitting around and around. Note that in circular knitting, your "rows" are now called "rounds." In order to knit in the round you will need to use circular needles, which will allow you to create a circle or a seamless tube. No need to sew seams! Hats, mittens, skirts, one-piece sweaters, socks, and handbags are just a few of the items that you may find knitted in the round. In this lesson we will learn about knitting in the round and try our hand at a few simple knit caps.

CIRCULAR NEEDLES

The magic of circular needles is that they can be used to knit back and forth (as you would with straight needles) or to knit in the round! We know many knitters who only use circular needles. Holding circular needles may take a bit of adjustment now that you've gotten used to holding straight needles, but once you get used to the circulars you will most likely come to love them.

Here's how to knit in the round:

1. Cast on to circular needles the same way you cast on to straight needles and place a stitch marker on your needle to indicate the beginning of a new round.

2. Slide the stitches evenly around the circular needle so that the *first* stitch you cast on is at the other end of your needles. Make sure that your stitches are not twisted on the needle.

3. Place the needle with the first stitch in your left hand and the needle with the yarn ball attached in your right hand. Begin knitting the first stitch and keep knitting all the way around until you reach the marker. You have just completed one round!

4. Slide the marker from the left needle to the right needle and continue knitting. If you stop and look at your work you will notice you are knitting one long spiral. How cool is that?

Reasons the Chicks love circular needles

1. Circular needles can be used in place of straight needles.
2. You won't need to keep as many different needles in your needle stash.
3. Since they don't have long ends, circular needles are very portable and fit neatly into a purse or laptop bag.
4. Their compact nature allows you to knit in close quarters: on an airplane or train, at a sporting event, in the car, or at the doctor's office.
5. If you use them to knit in the round, you won't have any seams to sew.

DOUBLE-POINTED NEEDLES

The concept of using double-pointed needles is basically the same as using circular needles: You are working in the round. The difference is that you will need to divide your stitches evenly (or as close to evenly as you can get) among three or four needles, using a spare needle to knit with. Using double-pointed needles allows you to work in very small rounds, so you can knit small, seamless items, such as socks, baby hats, mittens, gloves, and many other little projects. We will introduce you to using double-pointed needles in the following project.

Men's Crew Cap

CHICK FEED

Okay, if you saw two ladies in a hip skate-and-ski store measuring all the skull caps with tape measures . . . that was us. We wanted to make sure this cap had a really modern fit and feel. Our Men's Crew Cap is knitted in the round, beginning at the bottom and working up toward the crown.

Sizes

Large (X-Large)

Completed Measurements

18 (22)" circumference

Materials

~ 146 (228) yd/133 (208) m heavy
  worsted weight alpaca or wool
  blend yarn
~ Size US 7 16" circular needles
~ Set of 4 size US 7 double-pointed
  needles
~ Stitch markers
~ Finishing needle

Cap

Using size 7 circular needles, cast on 90 (95) sts

1. Work K1, P1, Rib Stitch Pattern for 4 rounds.
2. Work in St st (Knit every round) until panel measures 6" from beg.
3. Change to double-pointed needles, distributing stitches evenly over 3 needles.

Note: To change to double-pointed needles, just Knit the stitches off the circular needles onto the double-pointed needles, distributing the stitches fairly evenly among the three needles. Detailed instructions on how to use double-pointed needles begin below, on Round 14.

4. For size Large begin on Round 1, for size Small begin on Round 2.
- Round 1 *K17, K2tog*. Repeat from * to * around—90 sts.
- Round 2 Knit.
- Round 3 *K16, K2tog*. Repeat from * to * around—85 sts.
- Round 4 Knit.
- Round 5 *K15, K2tog*. Repeat from * to * around—80 sts.
- Round 6 Knit.
- Round 7 *K14, K2tog*. Repeat from * to * around—75 sts.
- Round 8 Knit.
- Round 9 *K13, K2tog*. Repeat from * to * around—70 sts.
- Round 10 Knit.
- Round 11 *K12, K2tog*. Repeat from * to * around—65 sts.
- Round 12 Knit.
- Round 13 *K11, K2tog*. Repeat from * to * around—60 sts.
- Round 14 Change to double-pointed needles. Using one double-pointed needle, knit the first 20 sts from your circular needle onto your double-pointed needle. Pick up a second double-point and knit the next 20 sts onto that needle. Pick up a third double-point and knit the remaining 20 sts onto that needle. You will no longer need your circular needles for this project.
- Round 15 *K10, K2tog*. Repeat from * to * around—55 sts. Following the decreases for this round, pick up the fourth double-pointed needle and knit stitches from the first needle onto it. You should now have an empty needle. Use it to knit the sts from needle two. When that needle is empty, use it to knit the sts from needle three, and so forth.

Note: When decreasing, you may find that one stitch is on one needle and the other stitch is on the next needle. Simply slide the stitches so they are right next to each other and can thus be knit together. The double-pointed needles serve the same purpose as circular needles, and it does not matter how many stitches are on each needle.

- Round 16 Knit.
- Round 17 *K9, K2tog*. Repeat from * to * around—50 sts.
- Round 18 Knit.
- Round 19 *K8, K2tog*. Repeat from * to * around—45 sts.
- Round 20 Knit.
- Round 21 *K7, K2tog*. Repeat from * to * around—40 sts.
- Round 22 Knit.
- Round 23 *K6, K2tog*. Repeat from * to * around—35 sts.
- Round 24 Knit.
- Round 25 *K5, K2tog*. Repeat from * to * around—30 sts.
- Round 26 Knit.
- Round 27 Bind off remaining sts.

Finishing

Note before finishing: Refer to Lesson 22, "Getting It All Together" (page 147), for instructions on various finishing techniques.

1. Sew top seam of cap using horizontal-to-horizontal mattress st.
2. Weave in all yarn ends.

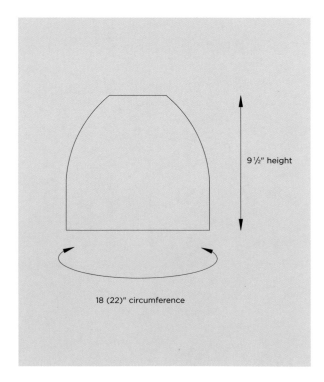

9½" height

18 (22)" circumference

Sorbet Striped Cap

CHICK FEED

We took just as much painstaking effort measuring hats at stores for this cap as we did for the Men's Crew Cap. This great-fitting cap can be knit in solid or stripes. We knitted ours in the round and from the bottom up to the crown.

Size
One size fits most

Completed Measurement
16" circumference

Materials
~124 yd/113 m worsted weight yarn in pink (A)
~75 yd/67 m worsted weight yarn in purple (B)
~75 yd/67 m worsted weight yarn in peach (C)
~Size US 7 16" circular needles
~Set of 5 size US 7 double-pointed needles
~Stitch marker
~Finishing needle

Abbreviation Key

beg	beginning
K	Knit
K2tog	Knit 2 stitches together
P	Purl
st(s)	stitch(es)
St st	Stockinette stitch

Sample was knitted in Classic Elite Lush (1.75 oz/50 g, 124 yd/113 m per ball; 50% angora, 50% wool) in Pink, Purple, and Peach.

Gauge
20 sts and 24 rows to 4" over St st (K 1 row, P 1 row) on size 7 needles, or size needed to obtain gauge

Stitch Guide:
K3, P3 Rib Pattern
~Row 1 Knit 3, Purl 3. Repeat across row.
~Row 2 Knit the Knit stitches and Purl the Purl stitches.
~Repeat Rows 1 and 2.

Cap

Using size 7 circular needles and color A, cast on 90 sts Place stitch marker on needle to designate beg of round, join round, being careful not to twist sts.

1. Work in K3, P3 Rib Pattern until piece measures 3" from beg.

2. Start changing colors: You will be alternating colors A, B, and C every 2 rounds working in St st (knitting every round will create St st when using circular needles).

3. Continue alternating 2 rounds of each color from here on, starting with color B.

4. When piece measures 4 1/2" from beg, change to double-pointed needles, distributing sts evenly over 4 needles.

Note: To change to double-pointed needles, just Knit the stitches off the circular needles onto the double-pointed needles, distributing the stitches fairly evenly among the four needles.

5. At this point you will now begin your decreasing rounds (K2tog).

- Round 1 *K16, K2tog*. Repeat from * to * around—85 sts.
- Round 2 Knit.
- Round 3 *K15, K2tog*. Repeat from * to * around—80 sts.
- Round 4 Knit.
- Round 5 *K14, K2tog*. Repeat from * to * around—75 sts.
- Round 6 Knit.
- Round 7 *K13, K2tog*. Repeat from * to * around 70 sts.

- Round 8 Knit.
- Round 9 *K12, K2tog*. Repeat from * to * around—65 sts.
- Round 10 Knit.
- Round 11 *K11, K2tog*. Repeat from * to * around—60 sts.
- Round 12 Knit.
- Round 13 *K10, K2tog*. Repeat from * to * around—55 sts.
- Round 14 Knit.
- Round 15 *K 9, K2tog*. Repeat from * to * around—50 sts.
- Round 16 Knit.
- Round 17 *K8, K2tog*. Repeat from * to * around—45 sts.
- Round 18 Knit.
- Round 19 *K7, K2tog*. Repeat from * to * around—40 sts.
- Round 20 Knit.
- Round 21 *K6, K2tog*. Repeat from * to * around—35 sts.
- Round 22 Knit.
- Round 23 *K5, K2tog*. Repeat from * to * around—30 sts.
- Round 24 Bind off remaining sts.

Finishing

Note before finishing: Refer to Lesson 22, "Getting It All Together" (page 147), for instructions on various finishing techniques.

1. Sew top seam of cap using horizontal-to-horizontal mattress st.

2. Weave in all yarn ends.

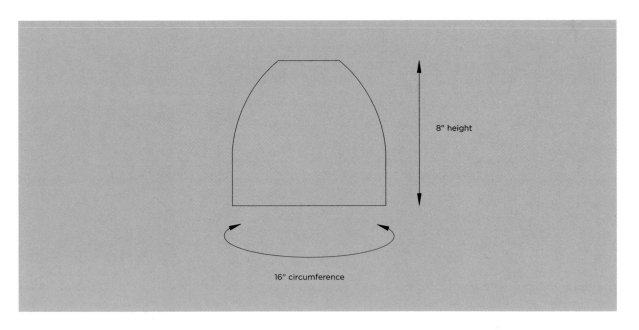

8" height

16" circumference

RIB IT,
JUST A LITTLE BIT

~~~~~~

BROKEN RIB STITCH

The Broken Rib stitch is another easy stitch. In a regular rib stitch, you always "Knit the knits" and "Purl the purls." This is a broken rib because the rib is only worked on every other row, so you'll have a Knit row and then a rib row. The end result is a great ribbed texture, but it does not have the tight stretch of a regular ribbed garment.

Here's how it's done:

~ Row 1 (right side) Knit.

~ Row 2 Purl 1, *Knit 1, Purl 1*. Repeat from * to * across row.

~ Repeat these 2 rows.

Metropolitan Pullover

CHICK FEED
Our Metropolitan Pullover is a great way to try your hand at knitting a garment with ribbed texture. This sweater has a relaxed fit and was knit with a chunky yarn, so you'll achieve results pretty quickly!

FLY THE COOP!
Try a neckline variation. We used a crochet edge on the neckline of this sweater, but instead you could pick up around the neckline with a circular needle and make a ribbed neck band.

Advanced Beginner

Sizes

Petite (Small, Medium, Large, X-Large, 1-X)

Completed Chest Measurements

32 (34, 36, 38, 40, 42)"

Materials

~ 825 (825, 900, 975, 975, 1,050) yd/754 (754, 822, 892, 892, 960) m heavy worsted weight yarn in red
~ Size US 10 ¹/₂ needles
~ Size J/6.0 mm crochet hook for finishing neckline
~ Finishing needle

Abbreviation Key

beg	beginning
dec	decrease
inc	increase
K	Knit
K2tog	Knit 2 stitches together
m 1	Make 1 (inc)
P	Purl
st(s)	stitch(es)
St st	Stockinette stitch

Sample was knitted using Classic Elite Duchess (1.75 oz/50 g, 75 yd/68 m per ball; 40% merino, 28% viscose, 10% cashmere, 15% nylon, 7% angora) in Red.

Gauge

14 sts and 25 rows to 4" over broken rib stitch on size 10 ¹/₂ needles, or size needed to obtain gauge

Stitch Guide:
Broken Rib Stitch Pattern

~ Row 1 (right side) Knit.
~ Row 2 Purl 1, *Knit 1, Purl 1*. Repeat from * to * across row.
~ Repeat these 2 rows.

Note

When you are increasing and decreasing, you must stay in the stitch pattern. Look at the stitch you are working and determine if it is a Knit stitch or Purl stitch (explained in Lesson 2, "The Chicks' Knitting Crash Course," page 29). This will help you decide which stitch you need to work next to keep your pattern consistent.

Back

Cast on 56 (60, 64, 66, 70, 74) sts

1. Work in Broken Rib Stitch Pattern until piece measures 13″ from beg.
2. Begin armhole shaping as follows: Bind off 2 (3, 4, 4, 5, 5) sts at beg of next 2 rows.
3. Dec 1 st (K2tog) at beg and end of every other row 2 (3, 3, 3, 4, 5) times.
4. Continue working in st pattern until piece measures 21 (21, 22, 22, 22, 22 1/2)″ from beg.
5. Bind off remaining sts in st pattern.

Front

Cast on 56 (60, 64, 66, 70, 74) sts

1. Work in Broken Rib Stitch Pattern until piece measures 13″ from beg.
2. Begin armhole shaping as follows: Bind off 2 (3, 4, 4, 5, 5) sts at beg of next 2 rows.
3. Dec 1 st at beg and end of every other row 2 (3, 3, 3, 4, 5) times.
4. Continue working in st pattern until piece measures 19 (19, 20, 20, 20, 20 1/2)″ from beg.
5. Begin neck shaping as follows: Work 17 (17, 18, 19, 19, 19) sts, attach a new ball of yarn. With new yarn, bind off center 14 (14, 14, 14, 14, 16) sts, complete the row. You now will be working both sides of the shoulders at the same time, each using its own ball of yarn.
6. Dec 1 st at each neck edge every other row 4 (5, 5, 5, 5, 5) times.
7. Continue working in st pattern until piece measures same as Back.
8. Bind off remaining sts in st pattern.

Sleeves (make 2)

Cast on 32 (32, 32, 36, 36, 36) sts

1. Work in Broken Rib Stitch Pattern, increasing as noted in step 2.
2. How to work inc row: Work 1 st, m 1, work to last st, m 1, work last st. You will be working inc row on rows noted: every 14th (14th, 11th, 14th, 12th, 10th) row 5 (5, 8, 5, 4, 10) times. Then inc every 15th (15th, 12th, 15th, 13th, 0) row 2 (2, 1, 2, 4, 0) times.
3. Continue working in st pattern until piece measures 17″ from beg.
4. Begin cap shaping as follows: Bind off 2 (3, 4, 4, 5, 5) sts at beg of next 2 rows.
5. Dec 1 st at beg and end of every 2nd (2nd, 2nd, 2nd, 2nd, 0) row 11 (6, 4, 4, 1, 0) times. Then dec 1 st at beg and end of every 3rd (3rd, 3rd, 3rd, 3rd, 0) row 2 (6, 9, 9, 11, 0) times.
6. Bind off remaining sts in st pattern.

Finishing

Note before finishing: Refer to Lesson 22, "Getting It All Together" (page 147), for instructions on various finishing techniques.

1. Sew shoulder seams together using horizontal-to-horizontal mattress st.
2. Sew sleeve top to armhole, easing to fit using vertical-to-horizontal mattress st.
3. Sew side and sleeve seams using vertical to vertical mattress st.
4. Single crochet around neckline for a finished look.
5. Weave in all yarn ends.

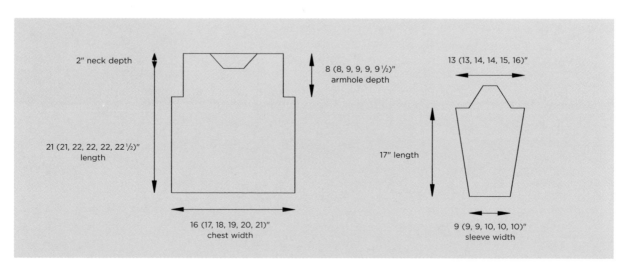

2″ neck depth

8 (8, 9, 9, 9, 9 1/2)″ armhole depth

13 (13, 14, 14, 15, 16)″

21 (21, 22, 22, 22, 22 1/2)″ length

17″ length

16 (17, 18, 19, 20, 21)″ chest width

9 (9, 9, 10, 10, 10)″ sleeve width

Lesson 16

TWIST AND SHOUT!

This lesson will be your first introduction to knitting cables. What is a cable? A cable is made by crossing stitches, which makes the yarn twist to achieve a very cool effect. Cables look best when knitted using a smooth yarn, to better show their dimensions. We'll show you the easiest cable to make, which doesn't even require using a cable needle.

TWISTED CABLE STITCH

The Twisted Cable stitch is really just a K2, P2 rib stitch with a twisted stitch every third row, and the outcome resembles a small cable. It is very easy to learn—just follow the pattern row by row.

Here's how it's done:

~ Row 1 (right side) Knit 2, *Purl 2, Knit 2. Repeat from * to end.

~ Row 2 Knit the Knit stitches and Purl the Purl stitches.

~ Row 3 Work the Knit stitches as follows: Knit 2 stitches together (do not slip these 2 stitches off the left-hand needle yet; reinsert the right-hand needle between these 2 stitches and Knit the first stitch again, slipping both stitches off the needle at the same time), then Purl the next 2 stitches. Repeat across row.

~ Row 4 Repeat Row 2.

~ Repeat these 4 rows.

Mock Cable Cami

Body

Cast on 124 (140, 156) sts

1. pm on needle to indicate beg of round, begin to knit, making sure your stitches are not twisted around needle.
2. Work in Twisted Cable Stitch Pattern until piece measures 15″ from beg.
3. Bind off loosely in st pattern.

Strap

Laying Body flat, measure approximately 2″ in from each outside edge of front and back of garment and place a locking stitch marker. With crochet hook, attach yarn at point in front where stitch marker is located and chain approximately 50 sts, or desired amount of sts for length of shoulder straps.

1. Chain 1 and turn, work 1 row of single crochet into chain.
2. Work 2 more rows of single crochet.
3. Attach to back of garment at stitch marker.
4. Repeat above directions for second shoulder strap.
5. Weave in all yarn ends.

Advanced Beginner

Sizes

Small (Medium, Large)

Completed Chest Measurements

32/34 (36/38, 40/42)″

Materials

~285 (380, 380) yd/260 (347, 347) m heavy worsted weight yarn in blue

~Size 9 24″ circular needles

~Locking stitch markers

~Size J/6.0 mm crochet hook for straps

~Finishing needle

Abbreviation Key

beg	beginning
K	Knit
P	Purl
pm	place marker
sl st	slip stitch
st(s)	stitch(es)
St st	Stockinette stitch

Sample was knitted in Twisted Sister Voodoo (1.75 oz/50 g, 95 yd/87 m per ball; 50% silk, 50% merino wool) in Indigo.

Gauge

16 st and 20 rows to 4″ over St st (K 1 row, P 1 row) on size 9 needles, or size needed to obtain gauge

Stitch Guide:
Twisted Cable Stitch Pattern

~Row 1 (right side) Knit 2, *Purl 2, Knit 2*. Repeat from * to * across row.

~Row 2 Knit the Knit stitches and Purl the Purl stitches.

~Row 3 Work the Knit stitches as follows: Knit 2 stitches together (do not slip these 2 stitches off the left-hand needle yet; reinsert the right-hand needle between these 2 stitches and Knit the first stitch again, slipping both stitches off the needle at the same time), then Purl the next 2 stitches. Repeat across row.

~Row 4 Repeat Row 2.

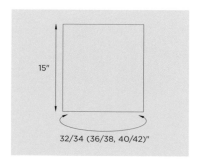

15″

32/34 (36/38, 40/42)″

CHICK FEED

This Mock Cable Cami project is a great way to try your hand at working the twisted cable stitch; it's a very easy, repetitive stitch, but if it still seems a little daunting, you may also work this pattern in 2 x 2 rib (K2, P2). There is no shaping to this simple garment; it's just a tube with straps.

SHAPING AND BUTTONHOLES

〜〜

REVERSE SHAPING

When a pattern calls for you to reverse the shaping, it is actually telling you to do the same thing you just did but to do it on the opposite side. This is usually the case when you are knitting the left and right sides of a cardigan. Pattern directions usually give directions only for one front side of the cardigan and then tell you to reverse the shaping for the other side.

The Chicks' trick is to lay the piece you have just knitted right side up on a table in front of you. Look at your piece. If your armhole shaping is on the right and the shaping for the neck is on the left, the next piece needs to have the armhole shaping on the left and the neck shaping on the right. Since you bind off only at the beginning of a row, when you work the pattern, your shaping will be off by one row. This is standard and will not impact your finished project. Voilà! You have just solved the mystery of the dreaded reverse shaping phenomenon! If you find that you need to mark on the pattern which side is which or which side you did first, definitely do so. That's one of the Chicks' cardinal rules: Make life easy!

BUTTONHOLES

We can't tell you how many times we've seen new knitters flipping through pattern books, longing to make a cardigan, but too afraid to make the buttonholes. We have good news! By this point in the book, you've already learned all the skills you need to make a buttonhole, so look on those cardigan patterns with a whole new confidence. We'll run through the two more traditional ways to make buttonholes.

Eyelet Buttonhole

The eyelet buttonhole uses a yarn over (which you learned in Lesson 13, "Over the Yarn We Go!," page 103) to create a hole and is done over one stitch. This method is very easy and is used for the following cardigan pattern. Just follow these steps. (The pattern you use will usually designate where to place the buttonholes.)

- Step 1 Knit (or Purl) until two stitches before the buttonhole.
- Step 2 Yarn over.
- Step 3 Knit (or Purl) the next two stitches together.
- Step 4 On the next row, Knit (or Purl) the yarn over as if it is a regular stitch.

One-Row Buttonhole

This method allows you to create buttonholes over a number of stitches. It is a horizontal buttonhole and is achieved by simply binding off the required number of stitches on one row. On the next row you will be required to cast the same number of stitches back on directly over the bound-off stitches. This creates a neat and firm buttonhole. We do not use this method in the projects in this book, but it is useful to know about the different methods.

Jackie Oh-So-Soft Sweater

CHICK FEED

Just like Jacqueline Onassis, the queen of chic, the Jackie Oh-So-Soft Sweater is very classic yet sophisticated. To make it more versatile, you can leave off the buttons (and buttonholes) and finish the edges with single crochet or a knitted border. Complete the look by using a decorative pin or simple tie to fasten in the front.

Advanced Beginner

Sizes

Petite (Small, Medium, Large, X-Large, 1-X)

Completed Chest Measurements

32 (34, 36, 38, 40, 42)"

Materials

~ 888 (1,036, 1,036, 1,184, 1,184, 1,332) yd/812 (947, 947, 1050, 1050, 1218) m light worsted weight mohair in blue
~ Size US 10 ¹/₂ needles
~ Size US 9 24" circular needles
~ 5 buttons
~ Finishing needle

Abbreviation Key

beg	beginning
dec	decrease
inc	increase
K	Knit
K2tog	Knit 2 stitches together
m 1	Make 1 (inc)
P	Purl
st(s)	stitch(es)
St st	Stockinette stitch
yo	yarn over

Sample was knitted in GGH Soft Kid Mohair (.88 oz/25 g, 150 yd/137 m per ball; 70% super kid mohair, 25% polyamide nylon, 5% wool) in Blue #63.

Gauge

18 sts and 20 rows to 4" over St st (K 1 row, P 1 row) on size 10 ¹/₂ needles, or size needed to obtain gauge

Back

With size 10 ½ straight needles, cast on 72 (76, 82, 86, 90, 94) sts

1. Knit 3 rows.
2. Change to St st, and work until piece measures 13" from beg.
3. Begin armhole shaping as follows: Bind off 3 (4, 5, 5, 6, 6) sts at beg of next 2 rows.
4. Dec 1 st (K2tog) at beg and end of every other row 3 (3, 4, 5, 5, 6) times.
5. Continue working in St st until piece measures 20 (20, 21, 21, 21, 22)" from beg.
6. Bind off remaining sts.

Front (right side)

With size 10 ½ straight needles, cast on 36 (38, 41, 43, 45, 47) sts

1. Knit 3 rows.
2. Change to St st and work until piece measures 13" from beg, ending with a right side row.
3. Begin armhole shaping as follows (you now will be on a Purl row): Bind off 3 (4, 5, 5, 6, 6) sts at beg of row, work remaining sts.
4. Dec 1 st at armhole edge every other row 3 (3, 4, 5, 5, 6) times.
5. Continue working in St st until piece measures 18 (18, 19, 19, 19, 20)" from beg.
6. Begin neck shaping as follows (neck shaping will be done on opposite side of armhole shaping): Bind off 8 (9, 9, 9, 9, 10) sts at beg of row, work remaining sts.
7. Dec 1 st at each neck edge every other row 6 (6, 6, 7, 7, 7) times.
8. Continue working in St st until piece measures same as Back.
9. Bind off remaining sts.

Front (left side)

With size 10 ½ straight needles, cast on 36 (38, 41, 43, 45, 47) sts

1. Knit 3 rows.
2. Change to St st and work until piece measures 13" from beg, ending with a wrong side row.
3. Begin armhole shaping as follows (you now will be on a Knit row): Bind off 3 (4, 5, 5, 6, 6) sts at beg of row, work remaining sts.
4. Dec 1 st at armhole edge every other row 3 (3, 4, 5, 5, 6) times.
5. Continue working in St st until piece measures 18 (18, 19, 19, 19, 20)" from beg.
6. Begin neck shaping as follows (neck shaping will be done on opposite side of armhole shaping): Bind off 8 (9, 9, 9, 9, 10) sts at beg of row, work remaining sts.
7. Dec 1 st at each neck edge every other row 6 (6, 6, 7, 7, 7) times.
8. Continue working in St st until piece measures same as Back.
9. Bind off remaining sts.

Sleeves (make 2)

With size 10 ½ straight needles, cast on 38 (38, 38, 40, 40, 46) sts

1. Knit 3 rows.
2. Change to St st, increasing as noted in step 3.
3. How to work inc row: Work 1 st, m 1, work to last st, m 1, work last st.

You will be working inc row on rows noted: every 8th (8th, 6th, 6th, 5th, 7th) row 8 (8, 9, 2, 2, 6) times. Then every 9th (9th, 7th, 7th, 6th, 8th) row 2 (2, 4, 10, 12, 5) times.

4. Continue working in St st until piece measures 17" from beg.
5. Begin cap shaping as follows: Bind off 3 (4, 5, 5, 6, 6) sts at beg of next 2 rows.

6. Dec 1 st at beg and end of every row 9 (6, 4, 4, 7, 1) times. Then dec 1 st at beg and end of every other row 7 (9, 12, 12, 10, 16) times.
7. Bind off remaining sts.

Finishing

Note before finishing: Refer to Lesson 22, "Getting It All Together" (page 147), for instructions on various finishing techniques.

1. Sew shoulder seams together using horizontal-to-horizontal mattress st.
2. Sew sleeve top to armhole, easing to fit using vertical-to-horizontal mattress st.
3. Sew side and sleeve seams using vertical–to-vertical mattress st.
4. Weave in all yarn ends.

Neck Band

1. Using size 9 circular needles (you will be using these needles as if they are straight needles, working back and forth) and with right side facing up, starting at right front neck, pick up approximately 62 (66, 70, 72, 72, 72) sts.
2. Knit 5 rows.
3. Bind off neatly.

Buttonhole Band (right side, as worn)

1. Using size 9 circular needles (you will be using these needles as if they are straight needles, working back and forth) and with right side facing up, starting at bottom edge pick up approximately 84 (84, 86, 86, 86, 94) sts.
2. Knit 3 rows.
3. Buttonhole Row: K5 (5, 4, 4, 4, 5), yo, K2tog, K17 (17, 18, 18, 18, 20), yo, K2tog, K17 (17, 18, 18, 18, 20), yo, K2tog, K17 (17, 18, 18, 18, 20), yo, K2tog, K17 (17, 18, 18, 18, 20), yo, K2tog, K5 (5, 4, 4, 4, 5).
4. Knit 3 more rows.
5. Bind off neatly.

Note: Remember that yarn overs are knitted as normal stitches.

Button Band (left side, as worn)

1. Using size 9 circular needles (you will be using these needles as if they are straight needles, working back and forth) and with right side facing up, starting at top edge pick up approximately 84 (84, 86, 86, 86, 94) sts.
2. Knit 7 rows.
3. Bind off neatly.
4. Sew on buttons as they correspond with buttonholes.

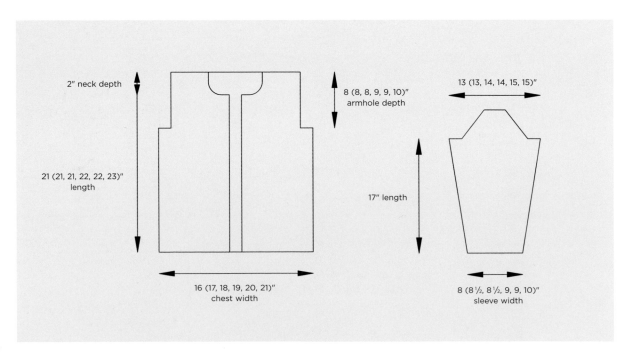

2" neck depth

8 (8, 8, 9, 9, 10)" armhole depth

13 (13, 14, 14, 15, 15)"

21 (21, 21, 22, 22, 23)" length

17" length

16 (17, 18, 19, 20, 21)" chest width

8 (8½, 8½, 9, 9, 10)" sleeve width

ADDING STITCHES

~~~~~~

CASTING ON TO THE TIP OF THE NEEDLE (AKA KNITTED CAST ON)

Occasionally a pattern will require you to cast on more stitches at the beginning and/or end of a row. For example, let's say you want to make a sweater in two pieces; just front and back, with the sleeves attached. If you start at the bottom edge and work upward, when you reach the arms you will need to increase stitches to create sleeves. This is done by casting on to the tip of the needle. The term "casting on to the tip of the needle" is actually a bit of a misnomer; it's really a knitted cast on, but is referred to as such because you are adding on to a work in progress. It's a fun way to create a sweater, and Nancy uses it often to knit simple sweaters for her daughter's stuffed animals.

Here's how to cast on to the tip of the needle:

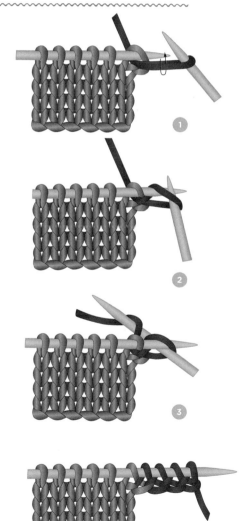

1. Knit the first stitch of that row, but do not take the newly formed stitch off the right-hand needle.
2. Twist and insert the left-hand needle under the front side of the new stitch on the right-hand needle and transfer that stitch to the left-hand needle (keep this stitch a little loose).
3. You just cast on the first stitch. Now insert the right-hand needle in this stitch and repeat the same steps for as many stitches as needed for your pattern.

CHEEP TRICKS

You can use this same process on a Purl row, so it doesn't matter that you are knitting on these stitches. The newly cast-on edge usually gets hidden in a seam.

The "Make Out" Sweater

Back

Using size 9 straight needles, cast on 79 (89, 99) sts

1. Work in Seed Stitch Pattern for 4 rows.
2. Change to St st, work for 7 (8, 8)".
3. Begin sleeve shaping: Cast on 3 sts to tip of needle for next 4 rows. Then cast on 4 sts at beg of next 2 rows.
4. Continue working in St st until the piece measures 14 (16, 16)" from beg.
5. Bind of loosely.

Front (left side)

Using size 9 straight needles, cast on 39 (45, 51) sts

1. Work in Seed Stitch Pattern for 4 rows.
2. Change to St st, work for 9 rows.

Sizes

Small (Medium, Large)

Completed Chest Measurements

0–32 (34–36, 38–40)"

Materials

~430 (585, 675) yd/393 (535, 617) m worsted weight yarn in white
~Size US 9 needles
~Size US 9 24" circular needles
~Size US 9 16" circular needles
~Finishing needle
~Stick pin (optional)

Abbreviation Key

beg	beginning
dec	decrease
K	Knit
K2tog	Knit 2 stitches togther
P	Purl
pm	place marker
st(s)	stitch(es)
St st	Stockinette stitch

Sample was knitted in Plassard Louinie (.88 oz/25 g, 43 yd/39 m per ball; 50% wool, 50% acrylic) in Ivory #027.

Gauge

20 sts and 26 rows to 4"over St st (K 1 row, P 1 row) on size 9 needles, or size needed to obtain gauge

Stitch Guide:

Seed Stitch Pattern

~Row 1 Knit 1, Purl 1. Repeat across row.
~Row 2 Purl the Knit stitches and Knit the Purl stitches.
~Repeat Row 2 until desired length.

CHICK FEED

It's Saturday night, you have a date with your special guy . . . so slip into this alluring little number. It's so soft, so fluffy, so easy—he won't be able to resist!

3. Begin neck shaping as follows: Dec 1 st (K2tog), at neck edge every 2nd row 8 (5, 2) times. Then dec 1 st at neck edge every 4th row 12 (15 18) times. AT THE SAME TIME, when the piece measures 7 (8, 8)" from beg, start sleeve shaping. Remember, use Knitting Shorthand (page 66) for this section.

4. Begin sleeve shaping as follows: Cast on 3 sts at sleeve edge 2 times. Then cast on 4 sts 1 time.

5. Continue working in St st until piece measures 14 (16, 16)" from beg.

6. Bind off loosely.

Front (right side)

Using size 9 straight needles, cast on 39 (45, 51) sts

1. Work in Seed Stitch Pattern for 4 rows.

2. Change to St st, work for 10 rows.

3. Begin neck shaping as follows: Dec 1 st at neck edge every 2nd row 8 (5, 2) times. Then dec 1 st at neck edge every 4th row 12 (15 18) times. AT THE SAME TIME, when piece measures 7 (8, 8)" from beg, start sleeve shaping. Remember, use Knitting Shorthand for this section.

4. Begin sleeve shaping as follows: Cast on 3 sts at sleeve edge 2 times. Then cast on 4 sts at each sleeve edge 1 time.

5. Continue working in St st until piece measures 14 (16, 16)" from beg.

6. Bind off loosely.

Finishing

Note before finishing: Refer to Lesson 22, "Getting It All Together" (page 147), for instructions on various finishing techniques.

1. Sew shoulder seams together using horizontal-to-horizontal mattress st.

2. Sew side and sleeve seams using vertical-to-vertical mattress st.

3. Weave in all yarn ends.

Front and Neck Band

1. Using size 9 24" circular needles and beg at lower right, pick up approximately 173 (197, 205) sts, working up right front side, around back of neck, and down left front side. (You will be working back and forth as if you are working on straight needles).

2. Work in Seed Stitch Pattern for 5 rows.

3. Bind off loosely in st pattern.

Sleeve Edge

1. Using size 9 16" circular needles, pick up approximately 63 (73, 73) sts around armhole edge.

2. pm to indicate beg of round.

3. Work in Seed Stitch Pattern in the round for 5 rounds.

4. Bind off loosely in st pattern.

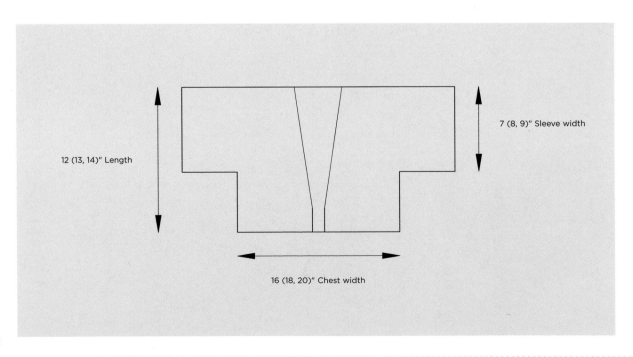

12 (13, 14)" Length

7 (8, 9)" Sleeve width

16 (18, 20)" Chest width

CABLE CONNECTION

Working a Cable

Cabling is what all those Aran Isle, fisherman knit sweaters have in common that makes them seem so magically beautiful. Chock-full of amazing texture and loaded with twists and turns, these sweaters can seem overly intricate and thus out of reach for the average knitter. But guess what? Those intricate-looking twists are called cables and they are actually very easy to make! Cabling is simply a technique of setting aside a few stitches to knit in different sequences. To do this, you'll need the help of a little tool called a cable needle, which conveniently holds those stitches until they need to be worked. Then you simply take the stitches, give them a twist, and tah-dah—cable made!

Here's how it's done:

1. Slip one or more stitches to a cable needle from the left-hand needle. These stitches will be held either in front or in back of your work (your pattern will state where these stitches need to be held).
2. Knit the next one or more stitches from the left-hand needle.
3. Knit the stitches off the cable needle.

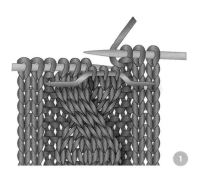

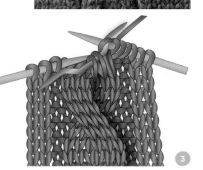

Twisted Tahoe Pullover

CHICK FEED

Don't be shy; give it a try! Just follow the pattern row for row, and it will guide you through. We've added our Knitting Flash Cards to this lesson to help walk you through garment shaping and tracking rows. As an alternative, this sweater may be knitted without the cable.

Advanced Beginner

Sizes

Petite (Small, Medium, Large, X-Large, 1-X)

Completed Chest Measurements

32 (34, 36, 38, 40, 42)"

Materials

~ 550 (550, 660, 660, 770, 770) yd/503 (503, 604, 604, 704, 704) m heavy worsted weight yarn in gray
~ Size US 10 ½ needles
~ Size US 10 ½ 16" circular needles
~ Stitch markers
~ Cable needle
~ Finishing needle

Abbreviation Key

beg	beginning
dec	decrease
inc	increase
K	Knit
K2tog	Knit 2 stitches together
m 1	Make 1 (inc)
P	Purl
pm	place marker
sl st	slip stitch
st(s)	stitch(es)
St st	Stockinette stitch

Sample was knitted in Plymouth Baby Alpaca Grande (3.5 oz/100 g, 110 yd/100 m per ball; 100% baby alpaca) in Gray #04.

Gauge

15 sts and 19 rows to 4" over St st (K 1 row, P 1 row) on size 10 ½ needles, or size needed to obtain gauge

Back

Using size 10 1/2 straight needles, cast on 60 (64, 68, 72, 76, 80) sts

1. Knit 4 rows.

2. Change to St st, work until piece measures 13″ from beg.

3. Begin armhole shaping as follows: Bind off 3 (3, 4, 4, 5, 5) sts at beg of next 2 rows.

4. Dec 1 st (K2tog) at beg and end of every other row 2 (3, 4, 4, 4, 5) times.

5. Continue working in St st until piece measures 21 (21, 21, 22, 22, 22 1/2)″ from beg.

6. Bind off remaining sts.

Front

Using size 10 1/2 straight needles, cast on 60 (64, 68, 72, 76, 80) sts

1. Knit 4 rows.

2. Change to St st and begin cable. The cable is worked over the center 12 sts on front side of sweater.

- Row 1 Set up row for cable: K24 (26, 28, 30, 32, 34), pm, P2, pm, K8, pm, P2, pm, K24 (26, 28, 30, 32, 34).

- Row 2 P24 (26, 28, 30, 32, 34), K2, P8, K2, P24 (26, 28, 30, 32, 34).

- Row 3 K24 (26, 28, 30, 32, 34), P2, K8, P2, K24 (26, 28, 30, 32, 34).

- Row 4 P24 (26, 28, 30, 32, 34), K2, P8, K2, P24 (26, 28, 30, 32, 34).

- Repeat Rows 3 and 4 another 4 times. (You should have 12 rows from beg.)

- Row 13 Work cable row: K24 (26, 28, 30, 32, 34), P2, slip next 4 sts on cable needle and hold in front of work, Knit next 4 sts, then Knit 4 sts off cable needle, P2, K24 (26, 28, 30, 32, 34).

- Row 14 P24 (26, 28, 30, 32, 34), K2, P8, K2, P24 (26, 30, 32, 34).

- Row 15 K24 (26, 28, 30, 32, 34), P2, K8, P2, K24 (26, 28, 30, 32, 34).

- Row 16 P24 (26, 28, 30, 32, 34), K2, P8, K2, P24 (26, 28, 30, 32, 34).

- Row 17 K24 (26, 28, 30, 32, 34), P2, K8, P2, K24 (26, 28, 30, 32, 34).

- Row 18 P24 (26, 28, 30, 32, 34), K2, P8, K2, P24 (26, 28, 30, 32, 34).

- Row 19 K24 (26, 28, 30, 32, 34), P2, K8, P2, K24 (26, 28, 30, 32, 34).

- Row 20 P24 (26, 28, 30, 32, 34), K2, P8, K2, P24 (26, 28, 30, 32, 34).

- Row 21 K24 (26, 28, 30, 32, 34), P2, K8, P2, K24 (26, 28, 30, 32, 34).

- Row 22 P24 (26, 28, 30, 32, 34), K2, P8, K2, P24 (26, 28, 30, 32, 34).

- Row 23 K24 (26, 28, 30, 32, 34), P2, K8, P2, K24 (26, 28, 30, 32, 34).

- Row 24 P24 (26, 28, 30, 32, 34), K2, P8, K2, P24 (26, 28, 30, 32, 34).

- Row 25 Work cable row: K24 (26, 28, 30, 32, 34), P2, slip next 4 sts on cable needle and hold in front of work, Knit next 4 sts, then Knit 4 sts off cable needle, P2, K24 (26, 28, 30, 32, 34).

3. Repeat Rows 14–25, until piece measures 13″ from beg.

4. Begin armhole shaping as follows (continue working cable pattern): Bind off 3 (3, 4, 4, 5, 5) sts at beg of next 2 rows.

5. Dec 1 st at beg and end of every other row 2 (3, 4, 4, 4, 5) times.

6. Continue working cable pattern until piece measures 19 (19, 19, 20, 20, 20 1/2)" from beg.

7. Begin neck shaping as follows: Work 17 (19, 18, 18, 19, 19) sts, attach a new ball of yarn. With new yarn, bind off center 16 (14, 16, 20, 20, 22) sts, work remaining 17 (19, 18, 18, 19, 19) sts. You now will be working both sides of the shoulders at the same time, each side using its own ball of yarn.

8. Dec 1 st at each neck edge every other row 3 (5, 3, 3, 3) times.

9. Continue working in St st until piece measures same as Back.

10. Bind off remaining sts.

Sleeves (make 2)

Using size 10 1/2 straight needles, cast on 34 (34, 34, 36, 38) sts

1. Knit 3 rows.

2. Change to St st, increasing as noted in step 3.

3. How to work inc row: Work 1 st, m 1, work to last st, m 1, work to last st.

You will be working inc row on rows noted: every 13th (13th, 8th, 8th, 6th, 8th) row 6 (6, 1, 6, 1, 6) times. Then inc every 0 (0, 10th, 10th, 8th, 10th) row 0 (0, 7, 3, 9, 3) times.

4. Continue working in St st until piece measures 17" from beg.

5. Begin cap shaping as follows: Bind off 3 (3, 4, 4, 5, 5) sts at beg of next 2 rows.

6. Dec 1 st at beg and end of every other row 2 (9, 4, 4, 4, 5) times. Then dec 1 st at beg and end of every row (3rd, 2nd, every, every, 2nd) row 7 (3, 2, 6, 7, 6) times.

7. Dec 1 st at beg and end of every 2nd (0, 0, 2nd, 2nd, 0) rows 2 (0, 0, 2, 2, 0) times

8. Bind off 2 (0, 2, 2, 2, 3) sts at beg of next 4 (0, 4, 4, 4, 4) rows.

9. Bind off remaining sts.

Finishing

Note before finishing: Refer to Lesson 22, "Getting It All Together" (page 147), for instructions on various finishing techniques.

1. Sew shoulder seams together using horizontal-to-horizontal mattress st.

2. Sew sleeve top to armhole, easing to fit using vertical-to-horizontal mattress st.

3. Sew side and sleeve seams using vertical-to-vertical mattress st.

4. Weave in all yarn ends.

Neck Finishing

1. Using size 10 1/2 circular needles and with right side facing up, begin at right shoulder and pick up approximately 59 (59, 59, 65, 65,73) sts around neck.

2. Purl 1 round.

3. Knit 1 round.

4. Purl 1 round.

5. Bind off loosely.

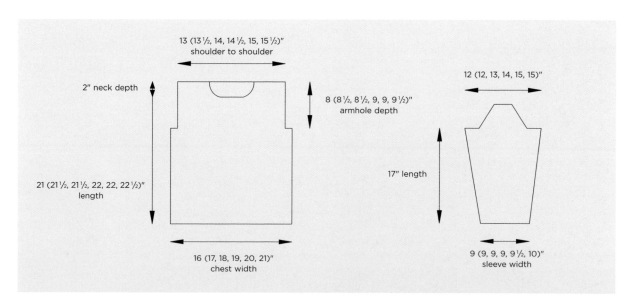

13 (13 1/2, 14, 14 1/2, 15, 15 1/2)" shoulder to shoulder

2" neck depth

8 (8 1/2, 8 1/2, 9, 9, 9 1/2)" armhole depth

21 (21 1/2, 21 1/2, 22, 22, 22 1/2)" length

16 (17, 18, 19, 20, 21)" chest width

12 (12, 13, 14, 15, 15)"

17" length

9 (9, 9, 9, 9 1/2, 10)" sleeve width

RAGLAN SHAPING

~~~~~~

WHAT IS RAGLAN?

If you live in or near the United States, chances are you have seen more than one baseball shirt. What makes this shirt style different from many others, including a T-shirt, is that the sleeve is cut at an angle and runs right up to the neck. Part of the sleeve top is actually attached at the neck (as opposed to a T-shirt, where the sleeve attaches to the shoulder seam), so keep that in mind when thinking about neck circumference. It is a very flattering look on many people (check out a few of those baseball players!).

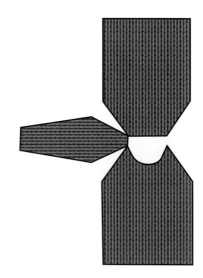

Knock-Around Hoodie

Back

Using size 13 straight needles, cast on 44 (48, 50, 52, 56) sts

1. Work in Seed Stitch Pattern for 4 rows.
2. Change to St st, work for 42 rows.
3. Begin raglan shaping as follows: Bind off 4 sts at beg of next 2 rows.
4. Dec 1 st (K2tog) at beg and end of every 3rd row 8 (6, 6, 4, 2) times. Then dec 1 st at beg and end of every 2nd row 3 (7, 7, 10, 14) times. Remember, use Knitting Shorthand (see page 66).
5. Bind off remaining sts.

Front (right side)

Using size 10 ½ straight needles, cast on 22 (24, 25, 26, 28) sts

1. Work in Seed Stitch Pattern for 4 rows.
2. Change to St st, work for 41 rows.
3. Begin armhole shaping as follows: Bind off 4 sts at beg of next row, work remaining sts.
4. Dec at armhole edge 1 st every 3rd row 8 (6, 6, 4, 2) times. Then dec 1 st at armhole edge every 2nd row 3 (7, 7, 10, 14) times. AT THE SAME TIME, when you have reached row 66 (68, 70, 70, 72), start neck shaping. Remember, use Knitting Shorthand.
5. Begin neck shaping as follows: Bind off 5 sts at beg of row, work remaining sts.
6. Dec 1 st at each neck edge every other row 2 (2, 3, 3, 3) times.
7. Bind off.

Sizes

Petite (Small, Medium, Large, 1-X)

Completed Chest Measurements

32 (34, 36, 38, 40)"

Materials

~600 (600, 800, 800, 800) yd/548 (548, 730, 730, 730) m super bulky weight yarn in cream
~Size US 13 needles
~Size US 13 24" circular needles
~Stitch marker
~5 toggle buttons
~Finishing needle

Abbreviation Key

beg	beginning
dec	decrease
inc	increase
K	knit
K2tog	Knit 2 stitches together
m 1	Make 1 (inc)
P	Purl
pm	place marker
st(s)	stitch(es)
St st	Stockinette stitch

Sample was knitted in Classic Elite Tigress (7 oz/200 g, 181 yd/166 m per ball; 100% wool) in Cream #7016.

Gauge

11 sts and 14 rows to 4" over St st on size 13 needles, or size needed to obtain gauge

Note

This pattern is a row-counting pattern, so an accurate gauge count is essential. A row counter might be useful in helping to keep track of your rows.

Stitch Guide:
Seed Stitch Pattern

~Row 1 Knit 1, Purl 1. Repeat across row.
~Row 2 Purl the Knit stitches and Knit the Purl stitches.
~Repeat Row 2 until desired length.

CHICK FEED

We're sure you'll find yourself putting on the Knock-Around Hoodie instead of your favorite old sweatshirt as soon as you finish it. We've designed it with raglan shaping to give it a relaxed, comfortable fit; used super chunky weight, self-striping yarn to make it a really fast knit and for the striping effect; and added a hood and simple toggle buttons to keep it trendy.

Front (left side)

Using size 10 1/2 straight needles, cast on 22 (24, 25, 26, 28) sts

1. Work in Seed Stitch Pattern for 4 rows.
2. Change to St st, work for 42 rows.
3. Begin armhole shaping as follows: Bind off 4 sts at beg of next row, work remaining sts.
4. Dec at armhole edge 1 st every 3rd row 8 (6, 6, 4, 2) times. Then dec 1 st at armhole edge every 2nd row 3 (7, 7, 10, 14) times. AT THE SAME TIME, when you have reached row 65 (67, 69, 69, 71), beg neck shaping. Remember, use Knitting Shorthand.
5. Begin neck shaping as follows: Bind off 5 sts at beg of row, work remaining sts.
6. Dec 1 st at each neck edge every other row 2 (2, 3, 3, 3) times.
7. Bind off.

Sleeves (make 2)

Using size 10 1/2 straight needles, cast on 24 (24, 26, 26, 26) sts

1. Work in Seed Stitch Pattern for 4 rows.
2. Work in St st, increasing as noted in step 3.
3. How to work inc row: Work 1 st, m 1, work to last st, m 1, work last st.

You will be working inc row on rows noted: every 11th (8th, 9th, 8th, 6th) row 4 (7, 4, 7, 7) times. Then inc every 12th (0, 10th, 0, 7th) row 1 (0, 2, 0, 2) times.

4. Continue working in St st until piece measures 17" from beg.
5. Begin cap shaping as follows: Bind off 4 sts at beg of next 2 rows.
6. Dec 1 st at beg and end of every 2nd row 3 (8, 8, 9, 13) times. Then dec 1 st at beg and end of every 3rd row 8 (5, 5, 5, 3) times.
7. Bind off.

Finishing

Note before finishing: Refer to Lesson 22, "Getting It All Together" (page 147), for instructions on various finishing techniques.

1. Sew shoulders to back using the horizontal-to-horizontal mattress st.
2. Sew sleeve top to armhole, easing to fit, using vertical-to-horizontal mattress st.
3. Sew side and sleeve seams using vertical-to-vertical mattress st.
4. Weave in all yarn ends.

Hood

1. Using size 13 circular needles and with right side facing up, pick up approximately 44 (46, 46, 46, 46) sts
2. P22 (23, 23, 23, 23), pm, work remaining sts.
3. Work in St st for 3".
4. Inc 1 st on each side of marker every 4th (6th, 5th, 5th, 5th) row 5 (5, 7, 7, 7) times. Then inc every 5th row 3 (5, 0, 0, 0) times.
5. Work until piece measures 13" from beg.
6. Bind off all sts.
7. Seam top using horizontal-to-horizontal mattress st.
8. If desired, you may single crochet around edge of hood.

Front Bands (left and right)

1. Using size 13 circular needles and with right side facing up, pick up approximately 54 (58, 60, 60, 62) sts along right front side.
2. Work in Seed Stitch Pattern for 5 rows.
3. Bind off loosely in st pattern.
4. Repeat steps 1–3 for left side.
5. There are no buttonholes worked into the front band; we found that a pointed toggle button slipped through the large stitches just fine. You also can attach a larger toggle to one side of the band and single crochet (see page 152) a loop on the opposite side to loop over the button if preferred.

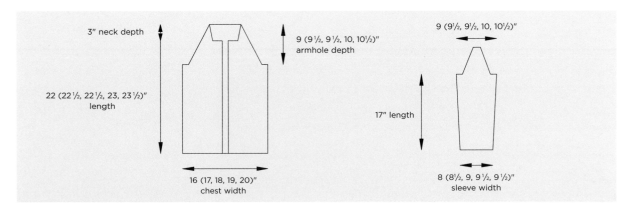

3" neck depth

9 (9 1/2, 9 1/2, 10, 10 1/2)" armhole depth

22 (22 1/2, 22 1/2, 23, 23 1/2)" length

16 (17, 18, 19, 20)" chest width

9 (9 1/2, 9 1/2, 10, 10 1/2)"

17" length

8 (8 1/2, 9, 9 1/2, 9 1/2)" sleeve width

LIFE *IS* FAIR!

Adding a little color to your knitting can really breathe life into it! Aside from using stripes there are two common ways to knit with color: Intarsia and Fair Isle. Here's how they are most commonly used.

INTARSIA

Intarsia is a technique in which blocks of color are worked with separate balls of yarn or bobbins. It also known as "picture knitting" because it is used if you want to create an emblem or motif in your pattern and it occurs only in specific place. For example, if you want to put one big heart on the front of a sweater, you would use the Intarsia method. Intarsia requires a different ball of yarn to be attached at each location that the color occurs; the yarns are then twisted around each other at each change to avoid holes in the pattern. The Intarsia method shouldn't be used circularly, however, as the yarns would end up in the wrong position. If you'd like to create a repetitive pattern of hearts all around a sweater, you would use the Fair Isle method, discussed next.

FAIR ISLE KNITTING

This method of knitting involves working with a few different colors of yarn across a row that is knitted and using a graph chart to form a color pattern. Colors alternate in a repeating pattern and unused colors are carried along the back, which are called "floats"; the end result is a very dense fabric. Fair Isle patterns usually do not work more than five stitches of any one color at a time. Stockinette stitch is most commonly used for Fair Isle because it is often knit in the round and allows the beautiful color work to show. When introducing a new color to a Fair Isle pattern, just tie the new color to the color you are using (1), drop the color you are using and start to knit with the new color. It sounds more complicated than it really is; in fact, you are just twisting the yarns together. In doing so you will need to know a few things to make this process a little easier.

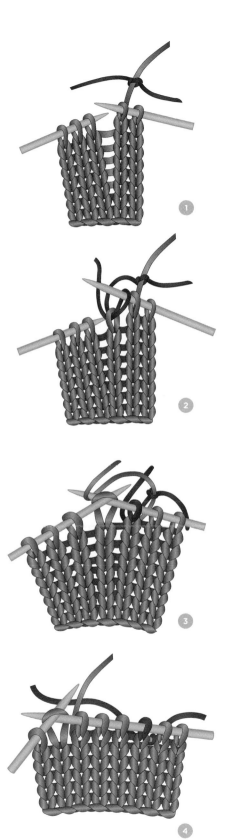

1. As you knit across the row, you will be alternating colors, plus carrying the spare yarn across the back by twisting the color not in use every four to five stitches, making sure that you do not pull the nonworking yarn too tight or it will cause your project to pucker.
2. Starting with color A, work across the row until you need color B; drop color A and pick up color B (2), leaving a 6″ tail of working yarn as when adding a new ball of yarn; start knitting with color B; when it is time for color A, drop color B and pick up color A, bringing it UNDERNEATH color B, and start knitting to the next color change. When you change colors again, bring the new yarn OVER the last color used (3), repeating this alternating process (4).
3. Trying to keep the different yarns from getting all tangled up can be somewhat frustrating. The Chicks find that measuring off a couple of yards at a time of your contrast colors and letting the yarn just hang in the back of your work is easier to maintain than a whole ball of yarn tangling around.

FOLLOWING A COLOR CHART

Read color charts upward from the lower right-hand corner. Follow odd-numbered rows from right to left, even-numbered rows from left to right. The color chart for the Men's Updated Argyle Golf Vest is found on page 158.

Men's Updated Argyle Golf Vest

CHICK FEED

Mary Ellen's husband has waited years for her to knit something for him. Her thoughts went something like, "He's a big guy . . . that would be a lot of knitting, and what if he doesn't like it?" We've known other knitters with the same complaint! Another problem is the lack of menswear knitting patterns on the market, so here's one for the guys. It's a simple vest, just two pieces! We added some coordinating diamonds on the front for an updated argyle effect.

Advanced Beginner

Sizes

Medium (Large, X-Large, XX-Large)

Completed Chest Measurements

40 (42, 46, 50)"

Materials

~ 981 (981, 1090, 1417) yd/897 (897, 997, 1295) m worsted weight yarn in gray (Main Color)
~ 109 yd/100 m worsted weight yarn in brown (A)
~ 109 yd/100 m worsted weight yarn in tan (B)
~ 109 yd/100 m worsted weight yarn in green (C)
~ Size US 7 needles
~ Size US 7 24" circular needles
~ Finishing needle

Abbreviation Key

beg	beginning
dec	decrease
inc	increase
K	Knit
K2tog	Knit 2 stitches together
m 1	Make 1 (inc)
P	Purl
st(s)	stitch(es)
St st	Stockinette stitch

Sample was knitted in Classic Elite Inca (1.75 oz/50 g, 109 yd/100 m per ball; 100% alpaca) in #1176, Gaucho Grey; #1114, Partridge; #1135, Moss; and #1142, Cajamaica Maroon.

Gauge

20 sts and 26 rows to 4" over St st (K 1 row, P 1 row) on size 7 needles, or size needed to obtain gauge

Stitch Guide:
K2, P2 Rib Pattern

~ Row 1 Knit 2, Purl 2. Repeat across row.
~ Row 2 Knit the Knit stitches and Purl the Purl stitches.
~ Repeat Rows 1 and 2.

Back

Using size 7 straight needles and Main Color, cast on 100 (104, 114, 124) sts

1. Work in K2, P2 Rib Pattern for 20 rows.
2. Change to St st, work until piece measures 17″ from beg.
3. Begin armhole shaping as follows: Bind off 5 (5, 7, 7) sts at beg of next 2 rows.
4. Continue working in St st until piece measures 29 1/2 (29 1/2, 29 1/2, 30)″ from beg.
5. Bind off remaining sts.

Front

Using size 7 straight needles and Main Color, cast on 100 (104, 114, 124) sts

1. Work in K2, P2 Rib Pattern for 20 rows.
2. Change to St st, work 39 more rows ending with a Purl row.
3. Work color chart (on page 158) as follows: Size 40 (42, 46, 50): Knit across first 8 (10, 15, 20) sts, then follow chart for next 84 sts. Then work last 8 (10, 15, 20) sts. Continue working in St st, incorporating the complete color chart.
4. Work until piece measures a total of 17″.
5. Begin armhole shaping as follows: Bind off 5 (5, 7, 7) sts at beg of the next 2 rows.
6. When piece measures 20 1/2 (20 1/2, 20 1/2, 21)″ from beg, begin neck shaping.
7. Begin neck shaping as follows: Work 45 (47, 50, 55) sts, attach a new ball of yarn. With new yarn, work remaining 45 (47, 50, 55) sts. You now will be working both sides of the shoulders at the same time, each side using its own ball of yarn.
8. Dec 1 st (K2tog) at each neck edge every 2nd row 16 (14, 20, 17) times, then every 4th (3rd, 3rd, 3rd) row 3 (6, 1, 6) times.
9. Continue working in St st until piece measures same as Back.
10. Bind off remaining sts.

Finishing

Note before finishing: Refer to Lesson 22, "Getting It All Together" (page 147), for instructions on various finishing techniques.

1. Sew shoulder seams together using horizontal-to-horizontal mattress st.
2. Sew side seams using vertical-to-vertical mattress st.
3. Weave in all yarn ends.

Neck Edging

1. Using size 7 circular needles, begin at lower right side of V-neck and pick up approximately 122 (122, 122, 142) sts, working up right front side, around back of neck, and down left front side, ending at V. Do not work in the round; you will be working back and forth, as if using straight needles.
2. Work in K2, P2 Rib Pattern for 1″.
3. Bind off loosely in st pattern.
4. Overlap ribbing at the V and sew in place using whip-stitch.

Armhole Edging

1. With size 7 circular needles, pick up approximately 136 (136, 144) sts around armhole edge.
2. Working in the round, work a K2, P2 Rib Pattern for 1″.
3. Bind off loosely in st pattern.

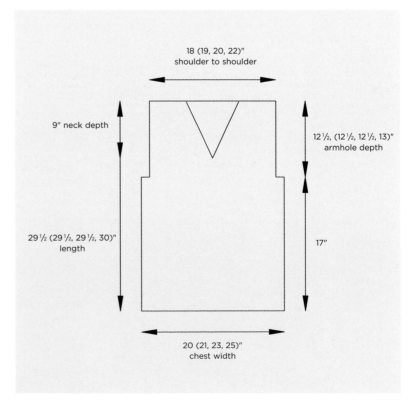

18 (19, 20, 22)″ shoulder to shoulder

9″ neck depth

12 1/2, (12 1/2, 12 1/2, 13)″ armhole depth

29 1/2 (29 1/2, 29 1/2, 30)″ length

17″

20 (21, 23, 25)″ chest width

GETTING IT ALL TOGETHER

Sewing and Finishing

Finishing is the grand finale of knitting. This art form that you have nurtured and devoted so much time to is finally starting to take shape. Learning to sew your garments together is a very important process of the whole knitting experience; and as with all aspects of knitting, it takes a little bit of time and practice but is definitely worth the effort. With a little pull here and a tug there, you'll end up with a garment that fits you like a glove. Good finishing techniques can mean the difference between an ultrastylish showpiece and a hopelessly home-made look.

BLOCKING

This process involves dampening or steaming the knitted pieces while they are shaped and smoothed by being pinned down into place on an ironing board or other flat surface to air-dry. Blocking reduces curling of the edges, making the pieces easier to sew together; it also will smooth out uneven stitches and can add inches to a knitted piece that was knit too small. However, some yarns today are purposely created to display the characteristics of uneven stitching. Also, some man-made fibers lose their appearance and quality if blocked, so read your yarn labels carefully before undertaking this step.

Wet Blocking

Wet the pieces either in a sink or in the washing machine, following the yarn manufacturer's instructions. Lay down the pieces on a padded surface, such as folded towels on a carpet or bed, and gently pat them into place, following the desired measurements. Pin down the pieces in place using rust-resistant straight pins and let them air-dry.

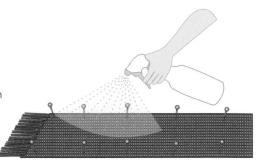

Steam Blocking

Pin down the edges of your pieces onto an ironing board so the pieces are shaped and flat. If you need a little more room than an ironing board provides, you may use folded towels on a carpet or bed; blocking boards are also available for your convenience. Using a good steam iron, hold the iron over the pieces, making sure not to let it touch the fabric, and release the steam evenly. Smooth your knitted pieces flat and then let them air-dry thoroughly.

Sweater Assembly

Once your knitted pieces are complete, it's time to sew them all together. It's very important to understand how a garment is assembled, since the process is the same for all the garment patterns in this book. Below are the basic sleeve assembly styles. Make a mental note of the following sequence, as it will take the guesswork out of which pieces need to be sewn together first:

1. Sew shoulder seams together.
2. Sew sleeve top to shoulder, easing sleeve to fit armhole.
3. Sew side seams from bottom edge to armhole.
4. Sew sleeves from sleeve edge to armhole.

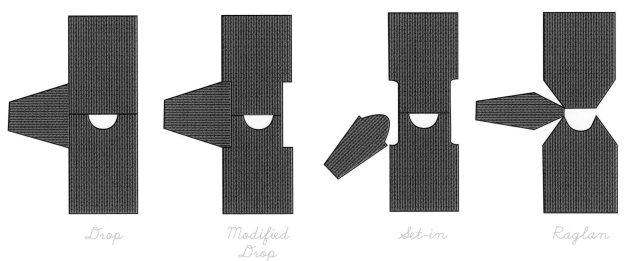

Drop   Modified Drop   Set-in   Raglan

INVISIBLE MATTRESS SEAMING

Garments are generally sewn together using what is called a mattress stitch, or invisible mattress seaming. The mattress stitch is always done with the right side of your knitted fabric facing up. This stitch will produce a smooth and invisible seam. There are two kinds of invisible mattress seams: vertical and horizontal. The differences between them and their specific uses are described below.

Quick Reminders

There are a few major points to keep in mind when you use invisible seaming on a Stockinette stitch:

- A Knit stitch in Stockinette stitch resembles the letter V.
- When using the horizontal method, you will be passing your finishing needle under the two strands of the V.
- When using the vertical method, you will be picking up two running bars in the middle of the V.

Shoulder Seams (Horizontal-to-Horizontal)

This seam is worked from the right side of the knitted fabric, and it joins two bound-off edges stitch by stitch. It is commonly used to stitch together shoulder seams. Here's how it's done:

CHEEP TRICKS

When seaming, keep your yarn tension even. Pulling the yarn too tightly will make the edges pucker, and they will not have the same drape as the rest of the knitted fabric.

1. Place the shoulder seams together at the bound-off edge with the right sides facing up.

2. Cut a piece of yarn approximately 18″ long and thread the yarn through the eye of the finishing needle.

3. Beginning at one side of the shoulder, insert the needle from back to front, attaching the yarn on the wrong side of the work and leaving a tail to be woven in later.

4. Working in the row below the bound-off row, pass the needle under the two strands of the V from one side of the shoulder, then pass the needle under the two strands of the V of the corresponding stitch from the opposite shoulder.

5. Repeat step 4 across the shoulder.

6. Secure the yarn to the back side of the shoulder seam and weave in the yarn end.

7. Repeat these steps for the opposite shoulder.

Adding Sleeves to the Body (Vertical-to-Horizontal)

This method is used when seaming the top of a sleeve to the edge of an armhole. With the right side of the knitted fabric facing up, you will be stitching the rows of the shoulder seams to the stitches of the sleeve top. Here's how it's done.

Fold the sleeve in half lengthwise to find the center of the top of the sleeve as follows:

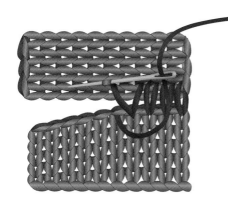

1. Place the sleeve top to the armhole with the right side facing up.

2. Cut a piece of yarn approximately three times longer than the length you are going to sew, and thread the yarn through the eye of the finishing needle. Attach the yarn to the wrong side of the shoulder and leave a tail to be woven in later. Bring the needle up through the middle of the shoulder seam, working one full stitch in from the edge stitch.

3. Beginning in the center point at the top of the sleeve, pass the needle under the two strands of the V from the top of the sleeve.

4. Now pick up the two strands from the middle of the V on the shoulder side.

5. Repeat steps 3 and 4, working down each side to the armhole edge, easing to fit.

6. Secure the yarn to the wrong side and weave in the yarn end.

7. Repeat these steps for the opposite sleeve and armhole shaping.

Side Seams (Vertical-to-Vertical)

This is an invisible seam worked vertically from the right side of the knitted fabric. It joins two edges row by row, and is used for joining side and sleeve seams. Here's how it's done:

1. Place the front and side seams together with the right sides facing up.
2. Cut a piece of yarn approximately 18" long, and thread the yarn through the eye of the finishing needle.
3. Attach the yarn to the wrong side of the bottom cast-on edge and leave a tail to be woven in later.
4. Working one full stitch from the edge stitch, pick up the two strands from the middle of the V on the front side of the garment, then pick up the two strands from the middle of the V from the back side of the garment.
5. Repeat steps 3 and 4 to the armhole shaping.
6. Secure the yarn to the wrong side and weave in the yarn end.
7. Repeat these steps for the opposite side.

Sleeve Seams (Vertical-to-Vertical)

1. Place the sleeve seams together with the right sides facing up.
2. Cut a piece of yarn approximately 18" long, and thread the yarn through the eye of the finishing needle.
3. Attach the yarn to the wrong side of the bottom edge of the sleeve cuff.
4. Working one full stitch from the edge stitch, pick up the two strands from the middle of the V on one side of the sleeve, then pick up the two strands from the middle of the V from the opposite side of the sleeve.
5. Repeat steps 3 and 4 to the armhole.
6. Secure the yarn to the wrong side and weave in the yarn end.
7. Repeat these steps for the opposite sleeve.

CHEEP TRICKS
It is a good idea to look over your seams every so often while stitching to make sure that your seams are neat and in a straight line and that your tension isn't too tight.

OTHER ASSEMBLY STITCHES

Seaming Garter Stitch

Place both pieces of knitted fabric side by side with the right sides facing up. Starting at the lower edge of one of the pieces and working with the existing tail or with a new piece of yarn, insert the finishing needle into the top loop on one side of the knitted fabric, then into the bottom loop of the corresponding stitch on the opposite side of the fabric. Continue in this manner until the seam is closed.

Whipstitch

Whipstitch seams are very flat, so they may be a good choice when joining shoulder seams of a bulky project. It's also very simple: With the right sides of the knitted fabric facing up, pass the finishing needle from back to front through one side of the knitted fabric, then from back to front on the opposite side. Continue in this manner until the seam is closed.

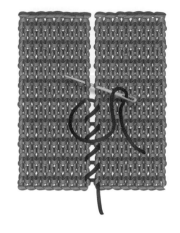

EDGING A GARMENT

Picking up stitches and adding collars and bands to your garment are the last steps in finishing off a project.

Single Crochet Edging

A single crochet stitch is a very handy stitch to learn, as it creates a nice, clean edge for almost any project. It works especially well around the necklines of sweaters.

1. Insert the hook one full stitch in from the edge of the knitted piece. Hook the new yarn and pull stitch through to right side.
2. Yarn over the hook and pull up a loop (two loops are on the hook), yarn over, draw the yarn through both loops on the hook (one loop is on hook).
3. Repeat steps 1 and 2 in the next stitch of the knitted piece, then repeat around the edge of your project.

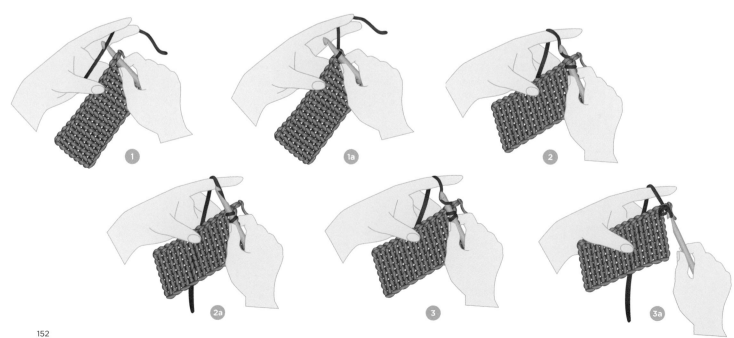

FIXING MISTAKES

"*UN*-KNITTING"

To rip, or not to rip . . . that is the question! It's happened to everyone: You're happily knitting along, thinking, "Hey, I'm getting pretty good at this knitting thing," when you look down and realize that you've dropped a stitch along the way, or you have too many stitches on your needle, or there's a hole in your knitting a few rows back. Momentary panic sets in. But take a moment to breathe: This does *not* mean that you need to rip out your entire project and start over from scratch! We've compiled a few quick fixes to the most common knitting mishaps, discussed below.

FIXING A MISTAKE IN THE SAME ROW

If you realize you made a mistake in the same row you're currently working, or one or two rows back, do not pull all the stitches off the needle and rip it out. Instead, you can use a handy little technique we call *Un*-knitting! It's like pressing the rewind button for knitting: You'll simply "rewind" back to the mistake, remove it, and then continue knitting where you left off. Here's how it's done:

Insert the left-hand needle into the stitch below the last stitch you made. Slide the stitch off the right-hand needle and pull out the yarn. Repeat until you reach the mistake.

CHEEP TRICKS

Sometimes you may lose or add stitches without realizing it. To avoid getting too far into the project before realizing that you don't have the right number of stitches on your needle, it is wise to get into the habit of counting your stitches every couple of rows. This will allow you to correct any errors more easily and prevent a lot of frustration.

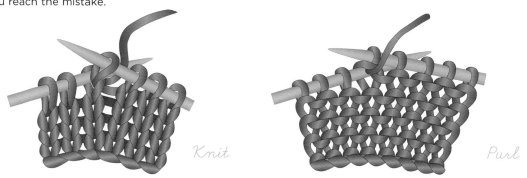

Knit   Purl

FIXING A DROPPED STITCH

A dropped stitch is really easy to fix if you catch it in the same row you are currently working. "Un-knit" (as shown on previous page) across to the dropped stitch. Insert the left-hand needle into the dropped stitch and then just pick it up and put it back on the needle. Here's how it will look, depending on the stitch you are using:

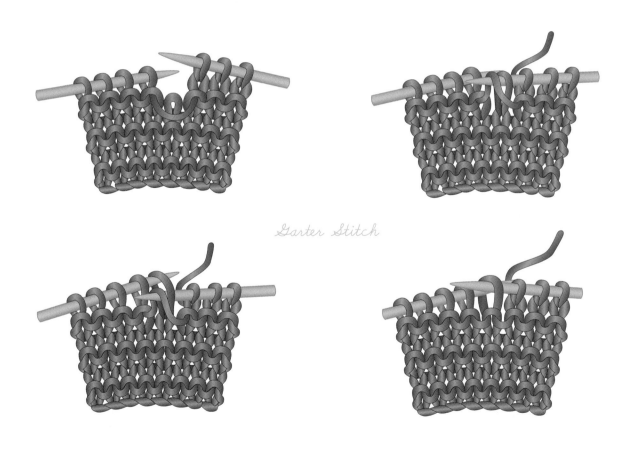

Garter Stitch

154

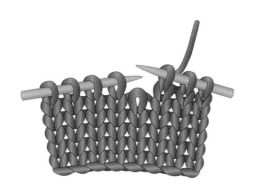
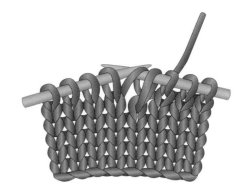

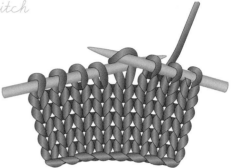

Stockinette Stitch

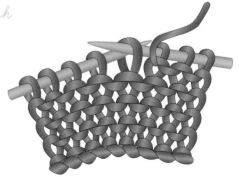

Purl Stitch

FIXING A RUN

Many women keep a bottle of clear nail polish in their handbag in case they get a run in their pantyhose. Just a little dab stops runs right in their tracks. As a knitter, you'll need to keep a crochet hook as your weapon of choice against those runs. How does a run happen? By dropping a stitch from your needle, which, if left uncorrected, will run all the way down to the beginning of your project, and you'll end up with a very wide hole.

If you dropped a stitch and it begins to run (meaning it unravels more than a row), you need to pick up the dropped stitch. First, use whatever implement you have handy to catch the runaway loop, such as an extra knitting needle, a safety pin, or even a piece of yarn. This will keep the dropped stitch from running through your project any further. Then, "un-knit" across the row to the point where the run began and continue as follows:

1. Using a crochet hook about the same size as your knitting needle, insert the hook from front to back into the dropped stitch.
2. Catch the lowest horizontal ladder from back to front for a Knit stitch and front to back for a Purl stitch and pull through the dropped stitch. Repeat these steps until you reach the top of the ladder. Place the dropped stitch back on the left-hand needle, making sure you don't twist the stitch when you do so.

FIXING EXTRA STITCHES

As we mentioned earlier, it's very important to count your stitches to make sure you are on track. Occasionally you may find that you've picked up an extra stitch or two. Why might this happen? Most of the time it's simply due to difficulty identifying individual stitches. Or you may have forgotten to slip a stitch all the way off your needle and accidentally knit it again; or you may have accidentally wrapped the yarn around the needle or picked up the yarn between stitches. Whatever the case may be, the more comfortable you become with knitting, the fewer mistakes you'll make in the end; and, if you do make a mistake, you'll have that much more confidence to fix it.

To fix extra stitches you have a few options:

1. You may "un-knit" back to the added stitch and remove it.
2. You can knit two stitches together at the end of the row.

FIXING HOLES

If you complete your project and realize that you have a hole in the middle of it, all is not lost! Here is a quick solution: Cut about a 6″ piece of yarn and loop it through the stitches that surround the hole; then pull the stitches together to close the hole and tie off and weave in the yarn end.

FIXING MISTAKES SEVERAL ROWS BACK

There will come a day when you look down at your project and notice a mistake WAAAYYYY back. If the mistake is likely to ruin your project by creating a large hole or run, you will need to rip out your stitches back to the mistake and fix it. It is horrific to think of all that lost work, but what's worse is having a completed project that you hate because you notice the mistake every time you look at it. Only you can decide if the mistake is "rip worthy." We find that new knitters hate to rip because each stitch was so painstaking to create in the first place. But the old saying "One step forward, two steps back" really applies. Ripping back is just part of the knitting process, and we've all had to do it at one point or another. But the good news is that you don't have to rip out your entire project—just to the point of the mistake. Here's how it's done:

1. Remove the stitches from the needle.
2. Pull out the rows until you reach the row with the mistake.
3. Carefully slip each stitch back onto the needle. Count the stitches on the needle to be sure you haven't missed any.
4. Continue knitting your project as normal and move on from the mistake!

Men's Updated Argyle Golf Vest
Color Chart

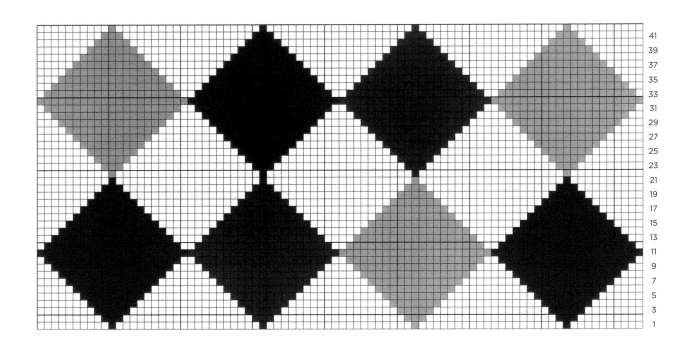

41
39
37
35
33
31
29
27
25
23
21
19
17
15
13
11
9
7
5
3
1

84 Stitches

Further Reading

There are a lot of great knitting books on the market. Many of them served as inspiration in our designs and stitch patterns and are must-haves for your knitting library:

The Complete Idiot's Guide to Knitting and Crocheting Illustrated, 3rd edition, by Barbara Breiter and Gail Diven (Alpha Books, 2006).

The Knitter's Handy Book of Patterns: Basic Designs in Multiple Sizes and Gauges, by Ann Budd (Interweave Press, 2002).

The Knitting Answer Book: Solutions to Every Problem You'll Ever Face, Answers to Every Question You'll Ever Ask, by Margaret Radcliffe (Storey Publishing LLC, 2005).

365 Knitting Stitches A Year: Perpetual Calendar, by the editors of Martingale (Martingale & Company, 2002).

Vogue® Knitting: The Ultimate Knitting Book, by the editors of *Vogue® Knitting Magazine* (Sixth&Spring Books, 2002).

Resources

Knitting Associations
The Knitting Guild Association (www.tkga.com)

Knitting Clubs & Communities
www.knitty.com
www.ravelry.com
www.thechickswithsticks.com